THE TEACHER'S RIGHT HAND

(A Resource Guide of Reading & Writing
Strategies, Lesson Plans, and Rubrics)

By

KIMBERLY RENA SHEFFIELD-GIBBONS
EDUCATIONAL CONSULTANT

1stBooks - rev. 06/12/01

TABLE OF CONTENTS

Dear Fellow Educators,

Time is a critical factor in all we do. We want our instruction to be effective as possible, but sometimes we do not have the time to put into planning, as we would like. This resource guide will offer easy to follow strategies and lesson plans that will save you some planning time as well as enhance your instruction.

As you know, many programs have been developed with the at risk learner in mind, and there are various programs created for the advanced learner. The strategies in this book are specifically designed for the average learner; however, they can be modified or enhanced to meet your students' needs.

I hope you will find the following pages filled with practical, time- saving ideas. Best wishes as you heed the call to educate our youth. May this resource guide truly be *your right hand.*

Cordially Yours,

Kimberly S. Gibbons
Author

CHAPTER 1:

READING STRATEGIES

Cynthia L. Chase
110 Arch St. #38
Keene, NH 03431

WHOLE GROUP: The following strategies work well with the entire class and only take 5—10 minutes to teach.

- **Kim's Version of Directed Reading Thinking Activity:** Teach students to use this strategy when reading any new material (story, expository text, news article, etc.). Have students do the steps below.

  1. Scan material—Read the title, subheads, questions, etc. Look at illustrations.
     Ask students: What do you think this selection will be about? Responses can be written or oral; however to make sure students grasp this strategy, have them respond orally the first few times you use it.
  2. Read first and last—Read silently the first sentence and the last sentence of the selection.
     Ask students: Do you have more clues about this selection? What are they?
     Responses can be written or oral.
  3. Read and think—Read parts of the selection orally. Be sure to stop and discuss. Ask students about main ideas and have them write and share their predictions. Continue reading and discussing until the selection is finished.

- **Popcorn:** This is a strategy that helps students stay focused on the reading assignment.

  1. Divide the class into two teams. The teacher can begin reading the selection or call on a student.

2. The reader reads at least two sentences but no more than a paragraph. After the reader finishes, he or she says, "Popcorn".
3. Then the reader will ask a student on the opposite team a question about what has just been read. If the response to the question is correct, one point is awarded to the team that gave the correct response.
4. The student, who responds to the question, then becomes the reader. If the answer is not known, the team loses a point. If no points have been earned, the team loses a turn to read.
5. The teacher should intercede when incorrect answers are given to make sure students have understood key points. Then, the teacher can call on a new reader.
6. Continue this strategy until the end of the reading selection, or the teacher can assign the class to read to a specific page or for a specific amount of time. Award the winning team!

- **ORC:** Oral Reading Comprehension will help students better comprehend main ideas in a reading selection.

  1. Divide the class into groups of four students. Give each group the same reading assignment.
  2. Have group members take turns reading orally sections of the assigned reading.
  3. After each member reads, the group will stop to discuss what has been read. Each reader will ask his or her own questions about what has just been read.
  4. After each group has finished the selection, have them make a quiz for another group to answer.
  5. Exchange the quizzes among the groups.

- **RSDW:** Read Silently, Discuss, and Write is another comprehension strategy. Students work with a classmate to improve their understanding of a reading selection.

  1. Time students as they read silently parts of an assigned reading selection (5-10 min.).
  2. When time is up, have students get with a partner and ask each other questions about the selection.
  3. Have the student pairs make notes about key points.
  4. Repeat steps 1—3 until the selection is finished.
  5. Have the student pairs write a summary of the selection.

- **Student as Teacher:** This comprehension strategy will help students learn content area material from a different perspective. The teacher trains students to teach. This may require some after school time to work with students.

  1. Assign 2 - 3 students a chapter to read on their own, and then schedule a day after school to meet with them.
  2. Have students explain the reading selection to you. Ask questions about the reading selection, and emphasize key points.
  3. Have students prepare their own lesson on the selection to teach to their classmates. This may take 2—3 days of after school planning with them.
  4. Students should teach the lesson to you before presenting it to their classmates.
  5. Have students teach their lesson. This is a great way to get students involved in their learning. Give each student an opportunity to teach during the year.

SMALL GROUP: These strategies should be taught in small group settings. They work best one on one, or with a group of two to four students. Try to work with each group at least 30 minutes a week. These strategies allow the teacher to address the student's individual needs.

- **Story Tellers Voice:** The purpose of this strategy is to help students with fluency. Try this strategy once or twice a month with each student. You will need a tape recorder, blank cassette, and headphones.

  1. Assign each student parts of a story, or content chapter to read orally.
  2. Tell students you want them to practice reading like a storyteller. Discuss expression, volume, speed, etc.
  3. The teacher should model reading for students, and then record each of them reading.
  4. After each reader has finished, rewind the tape.
  5. Have students put on their headphones and listen to the recording.
  6. The teacher and the students should make notes critiquing each reader.
  7. Give students some time to practice rereading their assigned section.
  8. Record students as they reread their assigned parts.
  9. Discuss student improvements and/or errors.

- **Reading Repetition Relay:** Repetition is another way to improve fluency. Encourage students to practice their oral reading by rereading stories, content chapters, etc.

  1. Have the students read silently a selection the class has previously read.
  2. Assign each student the same paragraph or section to read orally.
  3. Time each student during the reading and make notes regarding fluency, expression, errors, etc.
  4. Discuss observations with each student.
  5. Have students reread the paragraph while the teacher again makes notes.
  6. Give a point to the student who improved the most.
  7. Continue steps 1—6 assigning a new section of the reading selection.
  8. Award the student who received the most points.

- **Date With the Teacher:** This is a great way to give students one—on—one attention.

  1. Schedule a day of the week to meet with each student.
  2. When students are working independently, have the scheduled student to read orally to you. Have a special place set up in the classroom for the teacher and student to meet.
  3. Let the student choose the reading material (library book, magazine article, poem, etc.).
  4. Have the student read for about 5 minutes.
  5. Encourage the student to share thoughts about the reading material.
  6. Try to schedule 5—6 students each day.

- **Partner to Partner:** Students will have the opportunity to share a book they are reading with a friend as well as have some social time.

  1. The teacher should pair up students and decide how long the pairs will remain partners. (I suggest about a week).
  2. One student will read orally his/her own book for 5 minutes.
  3. After reading, the student will ask his/her partner a few questions.
  4. The other student then reads for 5 minutes and asks questions.
  5. The teacher should monitor closely.
  6. After each pair has read, allow 5 minutes of social time to those who were on task.

CHAPTER 2:

WRITING STRATEGIES

WHOLE/SMALL GROUP: These strategies can be taught to the entire class or in small groups. Try at least two strategies during the week.

- **Student/Teacher Conference:** Schedule a writing conference with each student at least once a week.

    1. First discuss the writing rubric with the student.
    2. Read the student's writing to him/her as it is.
    3. Have the student tell you mistakes he/she heard.
    4. Discuss ways to correct the writing.
    5. Have the student make those corrections and then look at the rubric.
    6. Reread the paper and have the student stop you if something doesn't sound right.
    7. Have the student highlight errors and make corrections.
    8. The student then revises the paper on his/her own using the rubric as a guide.

- **Tech Time:** Use technology to teach students to edit/revise. The teacher will display student writing that has been word-processed. The class will critique the writing. Be sure to have the appropriate technology to display the writing. (Smart Board, adaptor for the TV, overhead projector- computer connection, etc.).

    1. Have students type a paragraph on an assigned topic one or two days before you teach students how to edit/revise. Make sure each student prints his/her copy as well as save it.
    2. Display student writing one at a time and have a volunteer read it.

3. Call on students one at a time to come to the computer and list the corrections that need to be made. Have students make a section below the writing for these corrections, and have them lists positive comments. Make sure students use the writing rubric as a guide.
4. Discuss the corrections made and ways to make the paper better.
5. Save the comments. The original writer will use these to revise the paper.

- **Highlighting:** This is a good way to teach students to revise. Choose one student's paper and make a nameless copy for each class member. For more anonymity, type the paper and then make copies. Try to do five papers at a time. Over a period of time, each student's paper should have been critiqued.

  1. Give each student the same copy of a paper along with a highlighter.
  2. Have each student proofread and edit the paper using the highlighter to identify errors.
  3. Have students make notes on the back of the paper about the errors they highlighted.
  4. Discuss the errors as a class.
  5. Model steps 2- 4 before allowing students to work independently.

- **Pair Rap:** Pair students to write and discuss. Students write individually on an assigned topic, but they bounce ideas off their partner. They also proofread and edit each other's paper. Use this strategy only when students have begun to emerge as writers. They will truly benefit from discussing their writing with a classmate.

CHAPTER 3:

GRAMMAR LESSON PLANS

This chapter is filled with grammar lesson plans that focus on key Georgia Quality Core Curriculum Standards. These lesson plans were designed with the visual and kinesthetic learner in mind. Each lesson plan suggests a way to begin and end the lesson.

Kimberly Rena Sheffield-Gibbons

<u>GRAMMAR LESSON PLANS</u>

TOPIC: Types of Sentences
OBJECTIVE: Identifies the types of sentences.
GEORGIA MIDDLE SCHOOL QCC: 6-1, 7-1, 8-1
AMOUNT OF TIME: 25—30 minutes
MATERIALS: 4 posters (each with a different type of sentence), poster strips (1 for each student), 8 poster strips (each labeled with the name of one type of sentence, make two labels for each type), 4 pair of scissors, 4 magazines

INTRODUCTION: Pass out the sentence posters to volunteers. Have each student read his or her sentence. Explain each kind of sentence.

1. Write examples on the board and have the class identify each kind of sentence. Have students tell you what each sentence does and what kind of punctuation mark goes at the end of the sentence.

2. Give four different volunteers a magazine and a pair of scissors. Tell students the kind of sentence to search for. Have them cut it out and display it for the class to see.

3. Group Game: Divide the class into groups of four students. Assign each group member a kind of sentence to write on a poster strip. Compile all sentences and mix well. Divide the class into two teams. Tape the sentence type poster strips on the wall. Put four strips in one section of the room for team one, and put the other four strips in a different section of the room for team two. Place a chair or student desk in front of each strip. Give each team member a sentence strip turned faced down. When you say go, players go to the appropriate chair and place the sentence strip in it and run to the end of the line. The next player can go when the preceding player reaches him or her. The first team to correctly place sentence strips wins.

CLOSURE: Have students turn to a selection in their literature textbook and copy two examples of each kind of sentence. Include the page number beside each sentence. You may want to assign all students a previously read story, or

8

one you will be reading. The number of sentences copied can be increased depending on ability levels.

REFLECTION: _____

_____
_____
_____
_____

Kimberly Rena Sheffield-Gibbons

NAME: _____ DATE: _____

KIND OF SENTENCE RUBRIC

DIRECTIONS: Read each statement below. Be sure your work includes all of the items listed. The number of points you can earn is written beside each statement. How 'bout that **100**! Did you get it? _____ Five point bonus if you predicted correctly.

- Declarative Sentence (5pts. total)
    1. Copied the words of the declarative sentences from the textbook correctly. (1pt.)_____
    2. Capitalized declarative sentences correctly. (1pt.)_____
    3. Punctuated declarative sentences correctly. (1pt.)_____
    4. Put page number of each sentence. (2pts.)_____

- Imperative Sentence (5pts. total)
    5. Copied the words of the imperative sentences from the textbook correctly. (1pt.)_____
    6. Capitalized imperative sentences correctly. (1pt.)_____
    7. Punctuated imperative sentences correctly. (1pt.)_____
    8. Put page number of each sentence. (2pts.)_____

- Interrogative Sentence (5pts. total)
    9. Copied the words of the interrogative sentences from the textbook correctly. (1pt.)_____
    10. Capitalized interrogative sentences correctly. (1pt.)_____
    11. Punctuated interrogative sentences correctly. (1pt.)_____
    12. Put page number of each sentence. (2pts.)_____

- Exclamatory Sentence (5pts. total)
    13. Copied the words of the exclamatory sentences from the textbook correctly. (1pt.)_____
    14. Capitalized exclamatory sentences correctly. (1pt.)_____
    15. Punctuated exclamatory sentences correctly. (1pt.)_____
    16. Put page number of each sentence. (2pts.)_____

- Appearance (10pts. total)
    1. Sentences are neat and readable. (5pts.)_____
    2. Sentences are written in cursive. (5pts.)_____

- Total Points: _____
- Comments: _____

GRAMMAR LESSON PLANS

TOPIC: Sentences/Non-sentences
OBJECTIVE: Writes simple sentences and avoids nonfunctional fragments.
GEORGIA MIDDLE SCHOOL QCC: 6-7, 7-7, 8-7
AMOUNT OF TIME: 25—30 minutes
MATERIALS: large index cards (one per student), or construction paper cut into large strips, markers, strips of notebook paper, scissors

INTRODUCTION: Give each student an index card or strip of construction paper. Have students write *sentence* on one side of the card, and then write *non-sentence* on the other side of the card.

1. Use the overhead to display a variety of sentences and non-sentences. Explain the difference between sentences and non-sentences.
2. Find sentences in your grammar TE to read orally to students. Students will hold up their sentence/non-sentence response card after each sentence is read.
3. Have students write five sentences and five non-sentences on their own paper. Cut sentences into strips, mix them up and exchange with a partner. Each student labels his or her partner's sentences with *S or NS*. Have students check the answers.

CLOSURE: Call on each student to give a sentence or non-sentence. The other students will identify the sentence by holding up their response cards.

REFLECTION: _____
_____
_____
_____
_____

SENTENCE/NON SENTENCE TRANSPARENCY

DIRECTIONS: Read each statement below, and identify each statement as a sentence or non-sentence.

1. Damien went to the fair with his friends.

2. Walking two miles each day.

3. On our way to the game.

4. My sister, Beverly, likes to read mystery novels.

5. Put the basket over there.

6. Raspberries and whip cream.

7. The computer is not turned on.

8. Hooray! We won the championship!

9. The girls in the yellow dresses.

10. How many fish did you catch?

SENTENCE/NON SENTENCE TRANSPARENCY
(ANSWER SHEET)

DIRECTIONS: S = Sentence/NS = Non—Sentence
(10 pts. each)

1. Damien went to the fair with his friends. **S**

2. Walking two miles each day. **NS**

3. On our way to the game. **NS**

4. My sister, Beverly, likes to read mystery novels. **S**

5. Put the basket over there. **S**

6. Raspberries and whip cream. **NS**

7. The computer is not turned on. **S**

8. Hooray! We won the championship! **S**

9. The girls in the yellow dresses. **NS**

10. How many fish did you catch? **S**

GRAMMAR LESSON PLANS

TOPIC: Parts of a Sentence
OBJECTIVE: Identifies the parts of a sentence.
GEORGIA MIDDLE SCHOOL QCC: 6-3, 7-3, 8-3
AMOUNT OF TIME: 25—30 minutes
MATERIALS: 3 poster strips (each with a sentence), notebook paper, scissors, and envelopes

INTRODUCTION: Begin the lesson by displaying the poster strips for students. Have volunteers read the sentences. After each strip is read, cut it into two parts. When all strips have been cut, ask students, "Why did I cut each sentence into two parts?" Explain that every sentence has two parts, a subject and a predicate.

1. Choose a few students to write a sentence on the board, and then have the students draw a line to separate the two parts.

2. Group Game: Divide the class into groups of four. Have each member write a sentence on a piece of paper. The group should then place all sentences in an envelope. Exchange envelopes among groups. Each member chooses a sentence and cut it into the two parts. The first group to do this correctly wins the game.

CLOSURE: Read sentences orally to the class. Reread one part of the sentence and have students identify the sentence part.

REFLECTION: _____
_____
_____
_____
_____

SENTENCES FOR ORAL READING

DIRECTIONS: Read each sentence orally to the class. Reread the underlined part of the sentence and have students identify whether it is a <u>subject part </u>or <u>predicate part</u>.

1. Our class <u>is going to the zoo on Friday.</u>

2. <u>The men in the black jackets</u> are secret service agents.

3. <u>The President of the United States</u> is the highest elected official in the country.

4. Brad Pitt and Tori Spelling <u>are popular actors among teenagers.</u>

5. <u>My favorite foods</u> are grilled chicken and shrimp.

6. Bob Barker <u>hosts a game show called "The Price is Right."</u>

7. Six Flags over Georgia <u>closes in October</u>.

8. <u>Vickie and Lynn</u> won tickets to Disney World.

9. Fredia and Ronda <u>are hosting the New Year's Eve party.</u>

10. The choir <u>will sing three songs in the Christmas parade.</u>

SENTENCES FOR ORAL READING
(ANSWER KEY)

DIRECTIONS: Read each sentence orally to the class. Reread the underlined part of the sentence and have students identify whether it is a subject part or predicate part.

1. Our class is going to the zoo on Friday.   **PREDICATE PART**

2. The men in the black jackets are secret service agents.   **SUBJECT PART**

3. The President of the United States is the highest elected official in the country.   **SUBJECT PART**

4. Brad Pitt and Tori Spelling are popular actors among teenagers.   **PREDICATE PART**

5. My favorite foods are grilled chicken and shrimp.   **SUBJECT PART**

6. Bob Barker hosts a game show called "The Price is Right."   **PREDICATE PART**

7. Six Flags over Georgia closes in October.   **PREDICATE PART**

8. Vickie and Lynn won tickets to Disney World.   **SUBJECT PART**

9. Fredia and Ronda are hosting the New Year's Eve party.   **PREDICATE PART**

10. The choir will sing three songs in the Christmas parade.   **PREDICATE PART**

GRAMMAR LESSON PLANS

TOPIC: Nouns
OBJECTIVE: Identifies the eight parts of speech.
GEORGIA MIDDLE SCHOOL QCC: 6-2, 7-2, 8-2
AMOUNT OF TIME: 30 minutes
MATERIALS: envelopes (4 per group), index cards (4 per student), markers

INTRODUCTION: Display magazine pictures of famous people, well-known places, things of importance, and abstract ideas. Categorize each as a person, place, thing or idea.

1. Give each student four index cards and have them write an example of a person, place, thing, and idea (one per card).

2. Take up cards and shuffle well.

3. Divide the class into groups of four. Give each group four envelopes and have each member label an envelope with the following headings: person, place, thing, and idea.

4. Pass out index cards and have groups sort the cards into the correct envelopes. The first group to do so correctly wins.

CLOSURE: Have students identify nouns from a selection in their literature textbook. Give students a specified amount of time to find as many nouns as they can. Have students label the nouns as person, place, thing, or idea. Award the student who finds the most nouns.

REFLECTION: _____
_____
_____
_____
_____

GRAMMAR LESSON PLANS

TOPIC: Verbs
OBJECTIVE: Identifies the eight parts of speech.
GEORGIA MIDDLE SCHOOL QCC: 6-2, 7-2, 8-2
AMOUNT OF TIME: 30 minutes
MATERIALS: action pictures, grammar textbook, magazines, scissors, glue, construction paper

INTRODUCTION: Begin the lesson by showing students pictures of people doing various actions (eating, walking, dancing, talking, etc.). Explain that action words are called verbs.

1. Call on volunteers to role-play or pantomime actions and have other students figure out the action.

2. Read and discuss examples of verbs in grammar textbook.

3. Verb Poster: Have students look through magazines and cut out ten action words. Each student will write a sentence using the action word. Sentences should be written on construction paper (with the action word glued into the sentence).

4. Discuss the Verb Poster Rubric with students before they begin to work independently.

CLOSURE: Call on volunteers to read sentences from their verb posters and have classmates identify the action words.

REFLECTION: _____
_____
_____
_____
_____

VERB POSTER RUBRIC

DIRECTIONS: Use the guidelines below as you create a poster of action words. The total number of points you can earn is listed beside each statement.

I.   Following Directions
   A. The student cut out ten action words = 10 pts. _____
   B. The student wrote a sentence using each action word = 10pts. _____
   C. The student glued each action word into the sentence = 10pts. _____

II. Mechanics
   A. The student wrote complete sentences = 10pts. _____
   B. The student capitalized sentences correctly = 10pts. _____
   C. The student punctuated sentences correctly = 10pts. _____

III. Appearance
   A. The student's poster is headed properly (name, date) = 10pts. _____
   B. The student's poster is neat and readable = 20pts. _____
   C. The student's poster shows creativity = 10pts. _____

TOTAL SCORE: _____

COMMENTS: _____
_____
_____
_____
_____

GRAMMAR LESSON PLANS

TOPIC: Pronouns
OBJECTIVE: Identifies the eight parts of speech.
GEORGIA MIDDLE SCHOOL QCC: 6-2, 7-2, 8-2
AMOUNT OF TIME: 15—20 minutes
MATERIALS: grammar textbook, cassette from literature kit

INTRODUCTION: Use the grammar textbook to point out pronouns and their function. Explain the difference between object pronouns and subject pronouns.

1. Have students read sentences from the grammar textbook and identify the pronouns.

2. Listening Activity: Have students listen to parts of a literature selection on tape and list the pronouns they hear. Discuss as a class.

3. Assign a practice page from the grammar textbook for students to complete independently.

CLOSURE: Call on students at random to list pronouns on the board and use each in a sentence.

REFLECTION: _____
_____
_____
_____
_____

Kimberly Rena Sheffield-Gibbons

GRAMMAR LESSON PLANS

TOPIC: Adjectives
OBJECTIVE: Identifies the eight parts of speech.
GEORGIA MIDDLE SCHOOL QCC: 6-2, 7-2, 8-2
AMOUNT OF TIME: 40 minutes
MATERIALS: Adjective poster (cut out words from magazines and glue to construction paper or poster board), glue, magazines

INTRODUCTION: Introduce this lesson by showing the students a poster of adjectives. Explain how an adjective works in a sentence.

1. Students will choose 5 adjectives from the poster and use in sentences.

2. Call on volunteers to read one of their sentences and explain who or what the adjective is describing.

3. Adjective Identification Game: Students will identify adjectives for points.
    - Divide the class into two teams. Select team captains who will keep up with the score as well as draw *lots* to see which team goes first.
    - Read sentences from the grammar textbook to each student. Students must identify the adjective(s) in each sentence.
    - Award one point per adjective identified.
    - If a response is incorrect, ask a member of the opposing team to respond.
    - The team with the most points wins the game.

CLOSURE: Close the lesson by calling on students to give an adjective phrase (black dog, bossy girl, energetic dancer, etc.).

REFLECTION: _____
_____
_____
_____
_____

GRAMMAR LESSON PLANS

TOPIC: Adverbs
OBJECTIVE: Identifies the eight parts of speech.
GEORGIA MIDDLE SCHOOL QCC: 6-2, 7-2, 8-2
AMOUNT OF TIME: 30 minutes
MATERIALS: Flashcards of adverbs

INTRODUCTION: Show one flashcard and have students pronounce the word. Begin with *ly* adverbs. Ask students: What do all these words have in common? Continue with other adverbs. Discuss adverbs and their function.

1. Pair students and have them write their own sentences using adverbs.

2. Have pairs write one of their sentences on the board, and have the other students identify the adverb(s).

3. Group Activity: Divide the class into groups of four and have each group choose a literature selection. Groups will scan the selection and list as many adverbs as possible.

CLOSURE: Choose sentences from your grammar TE, and read aloud to the class. Call on volunteers to identify the adverbs.

REFLECTION: _____
_____
_____
_____
_____

GRAMMAR LESSON PLANS

TOPIC: Conjunctions
OBJECTIVE: Identifies the eight parts of speech.
GEORGIA MIDDLE SCHOOL QCC: 6-2, 7-2, 8-2
AMOUNT OF TIME: 40 minutes
MATERIALS: Transparency sheets, overhead projector

INTRODUCTION: Write FANBOYS on the board and explain to students this is a mnemonic device to help them remember the conjunctions.

1. F = for
2. A = and
3. N = nor
4. B = but
5. O = or
6. Y = yet
7. S = so

1. Identify conjunctions from the grammar textbook. This can be written or oral.

2. Divide the class into groups. Give each group a transparency sheet, and have students create their own worksheet on conjunctions.

3. Allow each group time to use the overhead projector to share their worksheet. Let each group call on other students to complete their worksheet.

CLOSURE: Randomly call on students to name one of the conjunctions and use it in a sentence.

REFLECTION: _____
_____
_____
_____
_____

GRAMMAR LESSON PLANS

TOPIC: Contractions
OBJECTIVE: Identifies the eight parts of speech.
GEORGIA MIDDLE SCHOOL QCC: 6-2, 7-2, 8-2
AMOUNT OF TIME: 20 minutes
MATERIALS: index cards, markers

INTRODUCTION: Write a list of contractions on the board or overhead. Show students how this shortened form is made up of two words.

1. Have the students pair up and make their own contraction flashcards.

2. Pairs will then exchange their flashcards with another group, and identify the two words that each contraction represents.

3. Pairs will get their original flashcards back and write a sentence for each.

CLOSURE: Have volunteers read their sentences and call on other students to identify the contraction.

REFLECTION: _____
_____
_____
_____
_____

GRAMMAR LESSON PLANS

TOPIC: Interjections
OBJECTIVE: Identifies the eight parts of speech.
GEORGIA MIDDLE SCHOOL QCC: 6-2, 7-2, 8-2
AMOUNT OF TIME: 20 minutes
MATERIALS: newspapers, magazines, highlighters

INTRODUCTION: Begin the lesson by pantomiming a few interjections. For example, to pantomime *ouch*, you could pretend to be hammering and accidentally hit one of your fingers. Call on a student to identify the interjection. Allow this student to pantomime the next interjection.

1. Discuss how to punctuate interjections.

2. Let students practice identifying interjections from their grammar textbook. Have them record their responses on paper.

3. Newspaper Activity: Search through newspapers and/or magazines for interjections and highlight as many as possible. Award the student who finds the most interjections.

CLOSURE: Choose a few sentences from the newspaper and magazine articles students highlighted. Read the sentences orally and have volunteers identify the interjections.

REFLECTION: _____
_____
_____
_____
_____

CHAPTER 4:

LEARNING CENTERS

Learning centers are generally used in early childhood programs; however, this approach to learning can be very beneficial for middle school instruction. In this section, you will find unique student-focused activities.

When setting up your classroom for centers, do not have more than six at a time. If possible limit each center to four or five students. Centers should last 20—30 min., so be sure to give students enough work to fill that time. Use a bell or timer to signal the end and have students move to the next center.

Plan to have learning centers approximately three consecutive days. The day before you begin learning centers, go over the rules of each center very thoroughly. Post step by step directions at each center. Expect a little noise and a lot of excitement!

CENTER TOPICS

Below you will find topic ideas for your centers. Once you are comfortable with learning centers, ideas will come easy to you.

- LISTENING CENTER (student focused)—tests student's listening and comprehension skills.

- LITERATURE CENTER (teacher focused or student focused)—tests student's knowledge of literary elements and genres of literature.

- READING CENTER (student focused or teacher focused - strategies)—tests student's use of reading strategies and comprehension.

- WRITING CENTER (teacher-focused or student focused)—tests student's use of the writing process.

- COMPUTER CENTER (student focused)—tests student's use of technology. Students should spend time each week learning software and/or word processing.

- ART CENTER (student focused)—tests student's creativity and imagination.

- COMMUNICATION CENTER (student focused)—tests student's ability to work with others, and tests student's oral expression.

- REFERENCE/STUDY SKILLS CENTER (teacher focused or student focused) Tests student's research skills, and tests student's study techniques.

- CONTENT CENTER (teacher-focused or student-focused)—Centers can be given the title of the specific subject matter (Math Center, Science Center, etc.). Select an objective(s) from the chosen subject to have students master.

CENTER SUGGESTIONS

❖ A day or two before you have learning centers, write or type directions for each station. Staple directions to a manila folder and post at each station. Student work can also go inside this folder. Some centers may need additional folders for other materials.

❖ Have a sign in sheet at each station, so you and the students can keep up with the stations they have completed.

❖ Decide how you will grade student work. (rubric, student self-check, etc.) You may choose not to give a grade for the teacher-focused lessons. You must also decide whether or not you will record the grades from each center or record only an average.

❖ Try to grade assignments each day and return them at the end of center time the following day.

❖ Appoint three reliable students as teacher's aides. These students will be responsible for restocking each center when needed. They will help other students as needed, and they will help monitor the noise. Tell students they are not to interrupt the teacher while he/she is working with a small group. Teach them the phrase, "Ask three, then me." This means they are to ask the three appointed classmates for help before interrupting a teacher-focused lesson.

❖ Explain the difference between student-focused centers and teacher-focused centers. Have only one or two teacher-focused centers.

❖ Invite a parent or other volunteer to come to your classroom on center days to help you supervise.

❖ To maintain high interest, change center topics every week or every other week. Be creative! Invite adult volunteers to share their talents and crafts as a learning center.

LISTENING CENTER

FOCUS: Listening and responding to literature

GEORGIA MIDDLE SCHOOL QCC: 6 -13, 6 -16, 7 -13, 7 -20, 8 -13, 8 -20

MATERIALS: tape recorder, literature cassette, headphones

DIRECTIONS: This center will test how well you listen and comprehend. Read each statement below very carefully and follow the steps.

1. You will need your literature textbook, paper, and pen or pencil. The other materials are already in the center. The tape recorder is ready, and the headphones are already plugged in.
2. Put on a pair of headphones and turn in your textbook to page _____. You will follow along in your text as the cassette plays. Listen carefully.
3. The group leader will press play when each person is ready to begin.
4. Listen to the entire selection.
5. When the selection ends, the group leader will rewind the tape to the beginning of the selection.
6. Head a sheet of paper like the example below

    Name
    Date
    Listening Center

7. Inside this folder you will find questions. Read the directions and answer each question.
8. When you finish, place your answers inside the center folder.
9. Clean up your area before moving to the next center.
10. If you finish before time is called, get a book or magazine from the designated area and read silently.

LISTENING CENTER

FOCUS: Following oral directions

GEORGIA MIDDLE SCHOOL QCC: 6 -14, 7 -14, 8 -14

MATERIALS: Tape recorder, cassette, headphones

DIRECTIONS: This center will test how well you follow oral directions. Follow each step below.

1. You will need paper, and a pen or pencil. Other materials are already setup.

2. Head your paper like the example below.

   > Name
   > Date
   > Listening Center

3. Put on a pair of headphones. The group leader will press play when everyone is ready.

4. Listen to your teacher's voice and follow the directions.

5. When you finish, the group leader will rewind the tape to the beginning.

6. Place your paper inside the center folder.

7. Clean up your area before moving to the next center.

8. If you finish before time is called, get a book or magazine from the designated area and read silently.

<u>FOLLOWING DIRECTIONS</u>

DIRECTIONS: Below you will find a sample message that can be recorded for a listening center activity.

- ❖ Hi students, this is your favorite teacher Mr./Ms. _____. I am going to see how well you can follow directions so listen carefully. Stop the tape after each direction so that you can respond. Do not rewind the tape to listen to a direction. Do not discuss with your group members.

- ❖ Draw a smiley face in the top right hand corner of your paper. Group leader please press stop and start the tape again when everyone is ready. Do not forget to stop the tape after each direction.

- ❖ Number your paper vertically 1—5. Do not skip lines.

- ❖ Beside each number you just wrote, write the first and last name of a famous person.

- ❖ Draw a circle around the first name of your favorite famous person you listed.

- ❖ Now number your paper 6—10 vertically. Do not skip lines.

- ❖ Beside numbers 6, 8 and 10, write the name of an animal.

- ❖ Beside numbers 7 and 9, write the name of an insect.

- ❖ On the last line of your paper, write your first and last name in cursive.

- ❖ You have completed this center activity. How well did you do? Make a prediction by writing a letter grade on the first centerline of the paper.

Thanks for your participation. Have a Super Day!

ART CENTER

FOCUS: Responding to literature creatively

GEORGIA MIDDLE SCHOOL QCC: 6-23, 6-30, 7-22, 7-29, 8-22, 8-29

MATERIALS: construction paper, markers, crayons

DIRECTIONS: You will use your imagination and creative skills to draw a scene from a story.

1. Turn in your textbook to page _____. Scan back over this story.

2. Choose your favorite scene and draw a picture on the construction paper using markers, crayons, etc. Save room for writing.

3. Write a few sentences summarizing the scene you drew.

4. When you are finished, head the back of your paper like the example below.

   Name
   Date
   Art Center

5. Place your work inside the center folder.

6. Clean up your area before moving to the next station.

7. If you finish before time is called, get a book or magazine from the designated area and read silently.

ART CENTER

FOCUS: Responding to literature creatively

GEORGIA MIDDLE SCHOOL QCC: 6-23, 6-30, 7-22, 7-29, 8-22, 8-29

MATERIALS: construction paper, markers, crayons, craft sticks, cardboard or poster strips, glue, index cards

DIRECTIONS: You will create your favorite character from a story.

1. Review the selection on page _____.

2. Choose your favorite character from this selection.

3. Using the materials provided, make a paper model of your favorite character. Be creative!

4. Glue the paper model to a craft stick and then glue another craft stick on the end of the first craft stick.

5. On an index card write a brief sketch of your character and tell why this character was your favorite.

6. Glue the index card to the second craft stick.

7. When you are finished, head the back of your index card like the example below.

   Name
   Date
   Art Center

8. Place your work inside the center folder.

9. Clean up your area before moving to the next station.

10. If you finish before time is called, get a book or magazine from the designated area and read silently.

READING CENTER

FOCUS: Reading strategies

GEORGIA MIDDLE SCHOOL QCC: 6-39 - 44, 6-49, 7-33 - 34, 7-37, 7-39 - 40, 7-43, 8-34 - 35, 8-38, 8-40 - 41, 8-44

MATERIALS: small dry erase boards, erasers, markers

DIRECTIONS: This center is teacher-focused. You will learn several reading strategies. Please follow the steps below before your teacher begins instruction.

1. You will need your literature or reading textbook, paper and pen or pencil.

2. Head your paper like the example below.

   Name
   Date
   Reading Center

3. Turn in your textbook to page _____.

4. Scan through the selection and list any unknown words on your paper.

5. Get a dry erase board, an eraser and a marker. Write one word from your list on the dry erase board.

6. Begin reading the selection silently. Your teacher will be with you shortly.

READING CENTER

FOCUS: Recognizing the difference between fiction and nonfiction

GEORGIA MIDDLE SCHOOL QCC: 6-34, 6-48, 7-38, 7-45, 8-39, 8-45

MATERIALS: excerpts from fiction and nonfiction

DIRECTIONS: You will read two articles and answer questions. Follow each step below.

1. Choose an excerpt from one of the folders labeled *fiction* or *nonfiction* and read silently.

2. Put the article back inside the folder.

3. Get a comprehension check from the appropriate folder in this center. It is printed on both sides. You will use the other side for your 2nd excerpt.

4. Read the directions and complete the comprehension check.

5. Choose an excerpt from the opposite folder and repeat steps 1—4.

6. Make sure your comprehension check has been headed correctly. Place your work inside the center folder.

7. Clean up your area before moving to the next station.

8. If you finish before time is called, get a book or magazine from the designated area and read silently.

READING CENTER: COMPREHENSION CHECK

DIRECTIONS: Fill in the blanks below.

NAME: _____

DATE: _____ CENTER: _____

1. Title of Article: _____

2. This article is fiction because _____
_____
_____
_____

3. Who is the main character and what is he or she like? _____
_____
_____
_____

4. What conflict did the main character face? _____
_____
_____
_____

5. How was the conflict solved? _____
_____
_____
_____

READING CENTER: COMPREHENSION CHECK

DIRECTIONS: Fill in the blanks below.

NAME: _____

DATE: _____ CENTER: _____

1. Title of Article: _____
    _____
    _____
    _____

2. This article is nonfiction because _____
    _____
    _____
    _____

3. This article was about _____
    _____
    _____
    _____

4. The most interesting part of this article was _____
    _____
    _____
    _____

5. I learned that _____
    _____
    _____
    _____

WRITING CENTER

FOCUS: Using a writing process

GEORGIA MIDDLE SCHOOL QCC: 6-69—70, 7-64—65, 8-64 - 65

MATERIALS: chart paper or small dry erase board, markers, eraser

DIRECTIONS: This is a teacher-focused center. You will learn how to prewrite, and you will learn how to draft a topic sentence. Follow the steps below.

1. You will need paper and a pencil. Head your paper like the example below.

   Name
   Date
   Writing Center

2. What comes to your mind when you think of Christmas? Make a list of words and/or phrases that make you think of this holiday. Try to list as many words as possible.

3. Please think of your own ideas, and work quietly.

4. Your teacher will be with you shortly to show you ways to prewrite and to teach you how to draft a topic sentence.

WRITING CENTER

FOCUS: Produces paragraphs for a variety of purposes

GEORGIA MIDDLE SCHOOL QCC: 6-70 - 73, 7-67—69, 8-67 - 69

MATERIALS: chart paper or small dry erase board, markers, eraser

DIRECTIONS: In this teacher-focused center, you will learn to draft a how to paragraph. Follow the steps below.

1. You will need paper and a pencil. Head your paper like the example below.

   Name
   Date
   Writing Center

2. Think for a moment about how to make a peanut butter and jelly sandwich. List everything that comes to your mind.

3. Your teacher will be with you shortly to teach you how to write the information from your list into a paragraph.

4. Please do your own work, and do not disturb others.

LITERATURE CENTER

FOCUS: Recognizes that literature reflects human experiences

GEORGIA MIDDLE SCHOOL QCC: 6-29, 7- 28, 8-28

MATERIALS: index cards, textbook or teacher-made scenarios

DIRECTIONS: You will empathize with characters as you role-play their actions. Follow each step below.

1. Choose one of the scenarios from the folder, and read it silently.

2. Get four index cards from the index cardholder.

3. Think about what each character might say or do and how each character might feel. You will now write the words/lines for each character mentioned in the scenario.

4. Proofread your work carefully.

5. Take turns reading your script to the other members in this center.

6. If there is time, choose the best script and role-play it.

7. Gem clip your index cards together. Head the back of the last card like the example below.

    > Name
    > Date
    > Literature Center

8. Place your work inside this folder.

9. Clean up your area before moving to the next station.

10. If you finish before time is called, get a book or magazine from the designated area and read silently.

<u>SCENARIOS</u>

DIRECTIONS: These scenarios can be used in centers or whole group lessons. Cut each scenario and glue to an index card. You can also laminate the cards.

❖ Gary, Mike, Tina and Julie are good friends who walk home together each day after school. One day the four stop at Dairy Queen for icecream. A man ahead of them in line drops a $10.00 dollar bill and doesn't realize it. Write out the words and actions that could take place.

❖ Tiffany and Alexia are invited to a costume party at the local teen center. When the girls arrive, they are shocked to find no one else dressed in costumes; instead, all other guests are dressed semi formal. How do you think these girls feel? What will they do? Write lines for each character.

❖ Brian and Kevin are neighbors and often borrow from each other. Brian cannot find his toolbox and remembers Kevin used it last. When he goes to get it back, Kevin confesses that he pawned the toolbox. Think about how each character might feel. Write what will happen.

❖ Your class has boarded the bus to see a production at the Fox Theater in Atlanta, Georgia. When the bus stops at a red light, a masked man with a rifle forces his way onto the bus. What will happen next? Write the script.

LITERATURE CENTER

FOCUS: Recognizes cultures and values represented in literature

GEORGIA MIDDLE SCHOOL QCC: 6-28, 7-27, 8-27

MATERIALS: copies of excerpts from short stories, biographies, poems, copies of reflection pages

DIRECTIONS: In this center, you will read an excerpt and write a response.

1. Choose an excerpt from the folder and read it silently.

2. After reading the excerpt, place it back inside the folder, and get a reflection page.

3. Fill in your name, date and center, and then read the directions.

4. When you finish, proofread your writing carefully.

5. Place your work inside this folder.

6. Clean up your area before moving to the next station.

7. If you finish before time is called, get a book or magazine from the designated area.

<u>REFLECTION PAGE</u>

DIRECTIONS: Write your thoughts and feelings about what you just read. Include in your writing, your opinion of the values presented. As you reflect, write about the culture that was depicted and compare/contrast it to your own.

COMPUTER CENTER

- Teach a whole group lesson on using the software before having students work on it independently.

FOCUS: Uses technology

GEORGIA MIDDLE SCHOOL QCC: 6-80, 7-76, 8-75

MATERIALS: computers, business card paper

DIRECTIONS: You will be creating your own business cards using Microsoft Publisher. You have been given an introductory lesson on Microsoft Publisher. Follow each step below carefully.

1. Brainstorm ideas for a business (name, address, services you will provide).
2. From the *start menu* click on Programs and then click on Microsoft Publisher.
3. Select *business cards* from the list of options, and then view the different designs. Choose one design you like.
4. Click on *start wizard* and follow the on screen instructions.
5. After the wizard finishes, you are ready to begin typing your own information on the screen.
6. Print one copy and proofread it carefully.
7. Make changes if needed and print one final copy.
8. Head the back of your paper like the example below.

   Name
   Date
   Computer Center

9. Place your work inside the center folder.
10. Clean up your area before moving to the next station.
11. If you finish before time is called, get a book or magazine from the designated area and read silently.

COMPUTER CENTER

- Teach a whole group lesson on using the software before having students work on it independently.

FOCUS: Uses technology

GEORGIA MIDDLE SCHOOL QCC: 6-80, 7-76, 8-75

MATERIALS: computers

DIRECTIONS: You will draft a paper using Microsoft Word. Read and follow the steps below.

1. From the *start menu* click on Programs and then click on Microsoft Word.
2. Select the font (no cursive or fancy font). The size of your font should be 12 or 14.
3. Head your paper like the example below.

   Name
   Date
   Computer Center

4. Your topic is *My Favorite Holiday*. Brainstorm ideas and show this on your draft.
5. Draft a paragraph on this topic.
6. Proofread your paper and make necessary changes if needed.
7. Save your work and print one copy.
8. Place your work inside the center folder.
9. Clean up your area before moving to the next station.
10. If you finish before time is called, get a book or magazine from the designated area and read silently.

COMMUNICATION CENTER

FOCUS: Participates in dramatic activities

GEORGIA MIDDLE SCHOOL QCC: 6-61—63, 66, 7-56—58, 61, 8-56—58, 61

MATERIALS: index cards, literature textbook

DIRECTIONS: In this center you will be collaborating to write a short skit. Follow each step below.

1. Think about the literature selections your class has read this year. Which was your favorite? Decide as a group and choose a scene from this selection to act out.
2. Next, decide who will play each character and begin discussing ideas for the lines of each character.
3. Each group member should write his or her own character lines.
4. Use the index cards to make notes, write lines, etc. Head the index card(s) like the example below.

   Name
   Date
   Communication Center

5. When each person has finished writing his or her lines, share with each other, and offer suggestions or make comments.
6. If there is time, practice role-playing the scene.
7. You will practice and perform the skit at a later date.
8. Place your work inside the center folder.
9. Clean up your area before moving to the next station.
10. If you finish before time is called, get a book or magazine from the designated area and read silently.

COMMUNICATION CENTER

FOCUS: Participates in oral presentations

GEORGIA MIDDLE SCHOOL QCC: 6-64, 65, 7-59, 60, 8-59, 60

MATERIALS: index cards, podium, video recorder, videotape

DIRECTIONS: In this center you will be writing a persuasive speech. The students at your middle school would like to have a ten-minute break each day. You must present your speech to the school board. The steps below will guide you through this process.

1. Use the index cards to brainstorm reasons why students should have a break each day. Work as a group to write an introduction and a conclusion.

2. Then each group member should write a paragraph expounding on one of the reasons.

3. Each group member will read his or her paragraph to the others. Offer suggestions as needed.

4. You will practice again and present this speech at a later date.

5. Place your work inside the center folder.

6. Clean up your area before moving to the next station.

7. If you finish before time is called, get a book or magazine from the designated area and read silently.

REFERENCE CENTER

FOCUS: Retrieves information on a single topic from multiple sources

GEORGIA MIDDLE SCHOOL QCC: 6-55, 60, 7-50, 55, 8- 49, 55

MATERIALS: index cards, various sources (encyclopedias, books, magazines, etc.) You may want to put books on reserve in the media center as well as schedule days for students to work in the media center.

DIRECTIONS: You will do mini research in the media center. Read two different sources for your information. Carefully follow the remaining steps below.

1. Choose one of the questions from the center folder and get two index cards.
2. Head the back of your cards like the example below.
    Name
    Date
    Reference Center

3. Take this center folder, and go to the media center. You will look for the answer to the question you selected. You can use an encyclopedia, book, magazine, etc.
4. Read the information silently, and on one of your index cards, write a brief answer in your own words. Write the name of the source, publisher and copyright date. See example below.
    Source: World Book Encyclopedia
    Publisher: Field Enterprises, Inc.
    Copyright: 1977

5. Select another source and repeat step four.
6. Proofread your work carefully.
7. Be sure to put all materials back and return to your classroom.
8. Please enter the room quietly.
9. Put the center folder back in the reference center. Make sure your work is inside the folder.
10. Clean up your area before moving to the next station.
11. If you finish before time is called, get a book or magazine from the designated area and read silently.

REFERENCE CENTER RESEARCH QUESTIONS

DIRECTIONS: Below are sample questions that could be used in the reference center. It is best to use questions that relate to a topic of study. Glue the questions to a strip of construction paper.

❖ Research Topic: The Human Body
  Question—How many times does the average person breathe during the day?
  Question—What is the largest human organ? How much of your total weight does this organ make up?

❖ Research Topic: Presidents of the United States
  Question - Who was the first president to die while in office?
  Question—Which president's daughter had her senior prom in the White House? What was her name?

❖ Research Topic: African American Actors
  Question—Who was the first African American woman to win an Academy Award? What was the title of the movie?
  Question—Who won an Oscar for his role in the 1989 film *Glory*?

❖ Research Topic: Sports
  Question—Who was the first person to win the World Heavyweight Title three times?
  Question—Who became the fastest woman on earth during the 1960 Olympics? What was her nickname?

❖ Research Topic: Holidays
  Question—What is the only holiday recognized by common law?
  Question—What holiday comes from the English phrase *Christes Masse*? What does this phrase mean?

REFERENCE CENTER

FOCUS: Uses a research process

GEORGIA MIDDLE SCHOOL QCC: 6-52, 7-49, 8-46

MATERIALS: index cards, various biographies, encyclopedias and other sources, gem clips

DIRECTIONS: In this center, you will research a famous person of interest to you. Follow each step listed below.

1. Brainstorm and select a famous person you are interested in learning more about.

2. Get a few index cards. Write that person's name on one of your index cards. Get a Research Notes Guideline sheet. Do not write on this sheet.

3. Choose a book, encyclopedia or other source that has information on the person you selected and begin reading silently.

4. Make notes as you read. Do not copy! Use your own words.

5. Include in your notes the reference source you used (title of source, publisher, and copyright).

6. Head the back of one of your cards like the example below.

   Name
   Date
   Reference Center

7. Gem clip your note cards and place them inside the center folder. You will use them at a later date to draft a paper.

8. Clean up your area before moving to the next station.

9. If you finish before time is called, get a book or magazine from the designated area and read silently.

RESEARCH NOTES GUIDELINE SHEET

DIRECTIONS: As you research your favorite famous person, use this sheet as a guide to help you narrow your search.

Early Years
- Date of Birth
- Parents' Names
- Growing Up

Education/Early Career
- High School
- College or Professional Training
- Jobs

Awards/Recognition/Hobbies
- What made this person famous?
- What honors has this person received?
- What hobbies does this person enjoy?

Family Life
- Spouse/Significant Other
- Children
- Pet(s)

CHAPTER 5:

POETRY LESSON PLANS

In this section, you will find innovative ways to teach poetry to your students. Lessons include poetry games, projects, rubrics and tests. Suggestions are also given on how to incorporate music into teaching poetry. For additional research, a poetry bibliography is given at the end of the chapter.

POETRY LESSON PLANS

FOCUS: Comparing and Contrasting music and poetry

GEORGIA MIDDLE SCHOOL QCC: 6-18, 20, 7-15, 18, 8-15, 18

AMOUNT OF TIME: 30 - 45 minutes

MATERIALS: tape player, popular music cassette, copies of lyrics, copies of poems, literature textbook

INTRODUCTION: Introduce this unit of study by playing popular music for the class. Give each student a copy of the lyrics. Music by any of the following artists would be appropriate: Mariah Carey, Brittney Spears, Whitney Houston, Brandy. Ask students ahead of time about their favorite music. Listen to the lyrics before playing music for students.

1. Class Discussion: Use the questions below to guide the discussion.
    - How are poetry and music alike?
    - How are poetry and music different?
    - Can you think of any poems you have read that are similar to a song you have heard?
    - What do the lyrics of this song suggest?
    - Do you agree with the statements made in this song? Why or why not?

2. Give each student a copy of the *Poetry Reading Strategies* and explain how to analyze a poem.

3. Have students turn to page _____ in their textbooks and read the poem _____ silently. Guide students through analyzing this poem.

4. Group Activity: Divide the students into groups of three. Give each group a copy of the same poem. Have students discuss and analyze the poem using the *Poetry Reading Strategies*. Assign each student a role (reader, recorder, and presenter).
    - Reader will read the poem orally.
    - Recorder will write notes.
    - Presenter will share the group's thoughts with the class.

54

5. Give each group time to present their analysis of the poem.

CLOSURE: Close the lesson by playing another popular song. Have students make notes as they analyze the lyrics. Call on volunteers to share their thoughts.

REFLECTION: _____
_____
_____
_____
_____

POETRY READING STRATEGIES

DIRECTIONS: To analyze a poem, follow the steps listed below. Always read the poem at least two times before you try to analyze it.

- **QUESTION**—Ask yourself questions as you read the poem.
  - Who is the speaker?
  - What is the poem about?
  - What descriptive words are used in the poem?

- **CLARIFY**—Identify and look up any unknown words or figurative language.

- **LISTEN**—As you read the poem, listen for rhyme, rhythm, and repetition.

- **SUMMARIZE**—In your own words, tell what the poem means.

- **RESPOND**—Give your thoughts and feelings about the poem.

POETRY LESSON PLANS

FOCUS: Recognizes images in poetry

GEORGIA MIDDLE SCHOOL QCC: 6-75, 7-71, 8-71

AMOUNT OF TIME: 30 minutes

MATERIALS: imagery flashcards, literature textbook, sensory word list, sensory worksheet

INTRODUCTION: Write the following (or sentences of your own) on the board.

1. Chestnuts roasting on an open fire.
2. The white, fluffy puppy ran briskly along the sidewalk.
3. We had hot, fresh rolls for supper.

Explain that sensory/descriptive words give a mental picture. Have volunteers read the sentences and identify the sensory words.

1. Pass out the sensory word list and have students read it silently.
2. Tell students to choose three sensory words and use each in a sentence.
3. Call on volunteers to share their sentences and have other students identify the sensory words used in the sentences.
4. Give each student a sensory worksheet to complete independently.
5. Read the poem on page _____ and have students pick out the sensory words.

CLOSURE: Use the imagery flashcards to review with students. Display cards and call on students to identify sensory words.

REFLECTION: _____

_____

_____

_____

_____

<u>SENSORY WORD LIST</u>

miniature	roar	icy	buttery	ripe
lavender	whisper	silky	crisp	fresh
costly	crackle	slippery	sour	spoiled
gold	scream	sticky	bitter	smoky
crimson	rustle	oily	spicy	rotten
wretched	whine	frozen	bland	fruity

SENSORY WORKSHEET

DIRECTIONS: Read each sentence and underline the sensory word(s).

1) Mark has an itchy mosquito bite on his leg.

2) The pie had a tangy lemon flavor.

3) The moonlight was as clear as crystal.

4) Amy's home has a nice scent of garden flowers.

5) Lauren almost fell on a slippery piece of soap.

DIRECTION: Write each sensory word you underlined in the sentences above under the correct column below.

EXAMPLE: A <u>crimson</u> car <u>roared</u> down the street.

Sight	Hearing	Touch	Taste	Smell
Crimson	Roared			

Kimberly Rena Sheffield-Gibbons

SENSORY WORKSHEET: ANSWER KEY

DIRECTIONS: Read each sentence and underline the sensory word(s).

1) Mark has an <u>itchy</u> mosquito bite on his leg.

2) The pie had a <u>tangy</u> <u>lemon</u> flavor.

3) The moonlight was as <u>clear</u> as <u>crystal</u>.

4) Amy's home has a nice scent of <u>garden</u> flowers.

5) Lauren almost fell on a <u>slippery</u> piece of soap.

DIRECTION: Write each sensory word you underlined in the sentences above under the correct column below.

EXAMPLE: A <u>crimson</u> car <u>roared</u> down the street.

Sight	Hearing	Touch	Taste	Smell
Crimson	Roared			
		Itchy		
			Tangy, Lemon	
Clear, Crystal				
				Garden
		Slippery		

60

IMAGERY FLASHCARDS

DIRECTIONS: Glue each group of words to a sheet of construction paper to make flashcards.

- **SMOKED ROBUST HAM**

- **HOWLING WIND**

- **ROYAL BLUE SILK DRESS**

❑ **RED JUICY APPLE**

❑ **SHINY GOLD STAR**

POETRY LESSON PLANS

FOCUS: Responds creatively to literature, and writes concrete poems

GEORGIA MIDDLE SCHOOL QCC: 6-30, 7-29, 8-29

AMOUNT OF TIME: 60 minutes or two 30 min. class periods

MATERIALS: copies of the poem, *Seal*, by William Jay Smith, copies of the poem, *The Sidewalk Racer or On the Skateboard*, by Lillian Morrison, large print coloring book with flowers, animals, fruit, etc., markers, crayons

INTRODUCTION: Pass out copies of *Seal* and have students read it silently. Call on volunteers to read the poem orally. Discuss the images and how they help the reader see the subject of the poem.

1. Read and discuss The Sidewalk Racer or On the Skateboard.

2. Tell students that both poems are called concrete. Explain why and give the meaning of a concrete poem.

3. Display examples of concrete poetry. Read a few examples.

4. Show students some of the patterns in the coloring book. Let students choose a coloring book pattern or come up with one of their own. The pattern they select will be the subject of their poem. For example, if a student chooses a car, he will write a poem about a car.

5. Discuss the poetry rubric with the class.

6. Have students draft the words of the poem and then they can color and decorate their patterns.

CLOSURE: Have one or two volunteers explain concrete poetry and share their example.

REFLECTION: _____
_____
_____
_____
_____

EXAMPLES OF CONCRETE POETRY

What a beautiful flower you are!

Among all the plants you shine like a star.

The many colors you display

Any one of them will brighten my day.

O Rose, O Rose, do not wither apart.

Stay one more day and warm my heart.

Kimberly S. Gibbons
December 27, 2000

EXAMPLES OF CONCRETE POETRY

A bear is such a huge creature that causes fear.

Why is man so afraid to get near?

Is he scared of being gnawed by the sharp-edged teeth?

Or is it the danger of the bear's hug?

Whatever it is I'm not going near.

'Cause this is one creature that I really fear!

Kimberly S. Gibbons
December 27, 2000

EXAMPLES OF CONCRETE POETRY

School is the place I go to learn,

And try my best all A's to earn.

The teacher guides me through the day

Encouraging me to listen, not play.

As soon as the bell sounds for the day to end,

Instead of going home, I want to start the day again.

Kimberly S. Gibbons
December 27, 2000

<u>RUBRIC FOR CONCRETE POETRY</u>

TITLE OF POEM: _____

AUTHOR: _____

SCORING: Rate the items in each section according to the following scale.

       1 = Poor
       2 = Weak
       3 = Average
       4 = Good
       5 = Excellent

I.   Content (10pts. each)
    A. Is the writing interesting?
    B. Does the writing make sense? _____
    C. Are sensory images used to develop the topic? _____
    D. Do all the details stick to the topic? _____
    E. Do the ideas presented flow together? _____

II. Mechanics (5pts. each)
    A. Is the grammar correct?
    B. Are words capitalized correctly? _____
    C. Are all punctuation marks used correctly? _____
    D. Are words spelled correctly? _____
    E. Is the handwriting neat? _____

III. Creativity (5pts. each)
    A. Does the poem create visual images?
    B. Is the poem original? _____
    C. Has the poem been colored and/or decorated? _____
    D. Does the poem have at least six lines? _____
    E. Overall appearance of the poem _____

Total Points _____

COMMENTS: _____
_____
_____

POETRY LESSON PLANS

FOCUS: Recognizes common elements of poetry

GEORGIA MIDDLE SCHOOL QCC: 6-25, 7-24, 8-24

AMOUNT OF TIME: 30 minutes

MATERIALS: poetry selections that emphasize rhythm and repetition, cassette of dance music (*Sweat* by C & C Music Factory, *Power of Love* by Luther Vandross, etc.)

INTRODUCTION: Play a dance selection for the students and allow volunteers to dance. Discuss rhythm and its importance in the music as well as dancing. Explain rhythm as it relates to poetry.

1. Have the class read a poetry selection from the textbook. Discuss the rhythm.
2. The students can then write about the mood the rhythm suggests.
3. Choose another poem where repetition is emphasized. Discuss repetition.
4. Have students list repetitive words and/or phrases.

CLOSURE: Divide the class into groups of three and assign roles to each member.
- Reader—reads the poem to the group
- Recorder—writes the group's responses
- Checker—checks over responses for correct spelling and line numbers

Have groups read a poem from the textbook and list the words and/or phrases of repetition. Students should also list the line number of the repetition. Reward the first group to list all repetition correctly.

REFLECTION: _____
_____
_____
_____
_____

<u>POETRY LESSON PLANS</u>

FOCUS: Recognizes common elements of poetry

GEORGIA MIDDLE SCHOOL QCC: 6-25, 7-24, 8-24

AMOUNT OF TIME: 60 minutes

MATERIALS: rhyming words flashcards, copies of *Nature Is* and *The Four Seasons,* cassette of rap music (Rap artist like Curtis Blow, Run DMC, C & C Music Factory are some of the earlier rap artists whose lyrics are more appropriate for the classroom).

INTRODUCTION: Begin the lesson by playing a rap song. Discuss this unique style of music and how rhyme plays a key part in the lyrics. As students listen to another selection, have them list rhyming words.

1. Read poems from the textbook and have students identify the rhyming words.
2. Assign student pairs a poem to read together. Have the pairs list the rhyming words.
3. Discuss rhyme scheme using a transparency of the poem *Celery* by Ogden Nash.
4. Read another poetry selection and have students label the rhyme scheme.
5. Give students copies of Jack Prelutsky's *Nature Is* and *The Four Seasons*. Students will read and label the rhyme scheme of each poem.

CLOSURE: Play the poetry communication game. Give each student a rhyming word flashcard. Each card should have two rhyming words. Students must find the person who has a card that rhymes with theirs. The pair will get together and write a four-line poem. The rhyming words must come at the end of each line. Poems can be serious, humorous, or nonsensical. Give each pair time to share their rhyme poem.

REFLECTION: _____
_____
_____
_____
_____

POETRY TRANSPARENCY

CELERY

Celery raw

Develops the jaw,

But celery stewed

Is more quietly chewed.

-Ogden Nash-

CELERY

Celery raw	A
Develops the jaw,	A
But celery stewed	B
Is more quietly chewed.	B

-Ogden Nash-

<u>POETRY COMMUNICATION GAME:</u>
<u>RHYMING WORDS</u>

BAKE	SOON	HOSE	CALL
STAKE	NOON	NOSE	WALL
LAKE	SPOON	GOES	HALL
CAKE	MOON	ROSE	SMALL
GONE	BLACK	NIGHT	STABLE
ON	JACK	FRIGHT	ABLE
PHONE	TRACK	BRIGHT	CABLE
BONE	SACK	LIGHT	TABLE
CAR	STAY	DATE	BOAT
STAR	WAY	MATE	OAT
BAR	DAY	GRATE	COAT
FAR	MAY	HATE	GOAT
BLUE	SHOOK	SEA	BIG
SUE	COOK	TEA	FIG
GLUE	LOOK	HE	TWIG
DUE	BOOK	KEY	WIG
LEG	CHAIR	JOKE	RED
BEG	STAIR	COKE	DEAD
KEG	CARE	WOKE	HEAD
EGG	DARE	SPOKE	BED

POETRY QUIZ # 1

NAME: _____ DATE: _____

PART 1 - DIRECTIONS: Write the correct answer in each blank. (10pts. each)

1) _____ refers to words or phrases that appeal to the senses.

2) A poem in which the shape suggests its subject is called _____.

3) _____ is a genre of literature that expresses feelings and emotions, and it is different in appearance from other forms of literature.

4) The technique of repeating a sound, a word, or a phrase is _____.

5) _____ _____ is the pattern of rhyme at the end of a line.

PART 2 - DIRECTIONS: Your teacher will give you a poem sheet to use in answering each question below. (10pts. each)

6) Read the poem titled *Flint* and list the pairs of rhyming words.

7) What does the speaker say a flint does?

8) Label the rhyme scheme of *I Heard A Bird Sing*.

9) What does the speaker hear in *I Heard A Bird Sing*?

10) What does the speaker compare the rain to in *Rain Poem*?

BONUS: Write a four-line rhyming poem. Poem should be original. (5pts.)

POETRY QUIZ # 1: POEM SHEET

DIRECTIONS: You will use this sheet to answer Part 2 of the test. Read each poem carefully and follow the instructions on the test.

Flint

An emerald is as green as grass,
A ruby red as blood;
A sapphire shines as blue as heaven;
A flint lies in the mud.

A diamond is a brilliant stone,
To catch the world's desire;
An opal holds a fiery spark;
But a flint holds fire.

Christina Rossetti

Rain Poem

The rain was like a little mouse,
quiet, small and gray.
It pattered all around the house
and then it went away.

It did not come, I understand,
indoors at all, until
it found an open window and
left tracks across the sill.

Elizabeth Coatsworth

I Heard A Bird Sing

I heard a bird sing
In the dark of December
A magical thing
And sweet to remember.
"We are nearer to Spring
Than we were in September,"
I heard a bird sing
In the dark of December.

Oliver Herford

POETRY LESSON PLANS

FOCUS: Recognizes common elements of poetry

GEORGIA MIDDLE SCHOOL QCC: 6-25, 7-24, 8-24

AMOUNT OF TIME: 60 minutes

MATERIALS: simile flashcards, copies of poetry quiz # 1 poem sheet

INTRODUCTION: Start the lesson by showing the students some flashcards of comparison.

- My heart beats like thunder.
- Amy's lips are red as roses.
- Jamal's kitten is soft as feathers.
- The classroom was quiet as a mouse.

1) Explain that these comparisons are called similes. Write the meaning on the board along with other examples.
2) Have volunteers reread the examples and tell the two things that are being compared.
3) Pass out copies of poetry quiz # 1 poem sheet and have students look for similes in each poem.
4) Divide the class into groups of four and have each group create their own simile poster.
5) Let each group display their work in the hall.

CLOSURE: Pair students and give each pair a magazine or newspaper. Each pair will search for a simile and cut it out. Have each pair post their example on a bulletin board or large sheet of chart paper.

REFLECTION: _____

_____

_____

_____

_____

SIMILE FLASHCARDS

****

My  beats like .

****

****

Amy's  are red as .

****

****

Jamal's  is soft as .

****

****

The  is quiet as a .

****

SIMILE POSTER DIRECTIONS

1. Choose one member to get all materials: poster, magazines, newspapers, glue, markers and scissors.

2. Search for five different similes in the newspapers and/or magazines.

3. Arrange the similes on the poster and draw or cut out pictures to go with each. Be creative!

4. Proofread your work using the simile rubric.

5. Hang the poster in the hall.

6. Put materials back in place and clean up your area.

SIMILE POSTER RUBRIC

Group Members: _____

Date: _____

SCORING: Your poster will be scored using the criteria below.

- Follows directions =   45 pts.
- Works cooperatively =   30 pts.
- Creativity =   25 pts.

I. **Following Directions**
   A. The group cut similes from magazines and/or newspapers.   5pts. _____
   B. The group cut five different similes.   10pts. _____
   C. The group cut out or drew pictures to go with each simile.   25pts. _____
   D. The group put materials back and cleaned up their area.   5pts. _____

II. **Cooperative Learning**
   A. Group members used the democratic process in assigning roles.   10pts. _____
   B. Group members shared ideas and were polite to each other.   10pts. _____
   C. Group members stayed on task and encouraged each other.   10pts. _____

III. **Creativity**
   A. Similes were arranged neatly on the poster.   10pts. _____
   B. Drawings/Pictures were appropriate.   10pts. _____
   C. Overall appearance of the poster was well done.   5pts. _____

Total Points   _____

Comments: _____
_____
_____
_____

POETRY LESSON PLANS

FOCUS: Recognizes common elements of poetry

GEORGIA MIDDLE SCHOOL QCC: 6-25, 7-24, 8-24

AMOUNT OF TIME: 60 minutes

MATERIALS: copies of limericks, one or more tape recorders and blank cassette(s)

INTRODUCTION: Read orally to the class *Old Man and the Cow* by Edward Lear. Discuss the pattern of rhyme and explain this type of poetry.

1. Call on a student to read *Old Man of Peru* and discuss the pattern of rhyme.

2. Write an example of a limerick for the students.

3. Have the class brainstorm a subject and write a class limerick.

4. Give students time to write their own limericks.

CLOSURE: Let each student go into the hall or to the media center to record their limerick on tape. Play the cassette for the class.

REFLECTION: _____
_____
_____
_____
_____

<u>LIMERICKS</u>

Old Man and The Cow

There was and Old Man who said, "How
Shall I flee from this horrible Cow?
I will sit on this stile,
And continue to smile,
Which may soften the heart of that Cow."

Edward Lear

Old Man of Peru

There was an old man of Peru
Who dreamed he was eating his shoe.
He woke in the night
In a terrible fright,
And found it was perfectly true.

Author Unknown

POETRY LESSON PLANS

FOCUS: Recognizes common elements of poetry

GEORGIA MIDDLE SCHOOL QCC: 6-25, 7-24, 8-24

AMOUNT OF TIME: 60 minutes

MATERIALS: copies of couplets, chart paper, markers, flashcards and poetry game transparency

INTRODUCTION: Pass out copies of couplets and call on volunteers to read examples. Give the definition of a couplet.

1. Write class examples on various subjects.

2. Have students write their own examples and read them orally.

3. Play Win, Lose or Draw

CLOSURE: Choose a win, lose or draw flashcard and have student pairs go to the board and write a couplet in 60 seconds.

REFLECTION: _____
_____
_____
_____
_____

COUPLETS

I can't eat anything anymore.
My mouth is too swollen and too sore.

I lost my red dress shoe.
Can I borrow one from you?

People say there's no place like home.
So why are people always gone?

If a tree begins to sway,
You'd better get out of the way.

Author: Kimberly S. Gibbons

POETRY GAME: WIN, LOSE OR DRAW

1. Divide the class into groups of three. Each group member will fill one of the following roles: recorder, artist, and reader.

2. Draw *lots* to determine which group goes to the chart/drawing board first.

3. The chart/drawing board should be turned away from the students

4. The artist from the group chooses a flashcard and draws a picture of the word.

5. When the artist returns to his/her group, the teacher will turn the chart/drawing board to face the class.

6. Each group identifies the picture and begins writing a couplet about the subject. Students should not yell out the identity of the picture.

7. The recorder should write the words on paper, but each member should try to contribute ideas.

8. When the couplet is completed, the reader of the group should stand to let the teacher know your group has finished. Remember, your group is trying to finish first. The teacher will check the poem and award 1 pt. if the writing is correct. Then, the reader will share the poem with the class.

POETRY GAME: FLASHCARDS

FLAG    CAR

APPLE    ICE CREAM CONE

BALLOONS    TREE

POETRY GAME: FLASHCARDS

 BUS

TELEPHONE

FISH

DOG

 CAP

COMPUTER

POETRY QUIZ # 2

NAME: _____ DATE: _____

1. Define the term <u>simile</u> and write two examples. (25pts.)

2. A limerick is a five- line poem. Which lines rhyme with one another? (25pts.)

3. Write an example of a limerick. (25pts.)

4. What is a couplet? Write two examples. (25pts.)

POETRY PROJECTS

The projects listed below are a great way to close out a unit of study on poetry. Allow students plenty of time to prepare their projects.

❑ Poetry Booklets—Have students create their own booklets.

❑ Student Poetry Recital - Invite guests and serve refreshments.

❑ Dramatizations—Act out favorite poems.

❑ Class poetry contest - Invite business partners to read and judge student poems

❑ Poetry Fest - Get the entire school involved in an evening event, display student poetry, invite the community (local poets, musicians) have readings, recitals, dramatizations, etc.

POETRY RESOURCES

Have a variety of poetry books available for your students to read. Below are some student favorites.

Bryan, Ashley. (1997). Ashley Bryan's A B C of African American Poetry. Atheneum Books for Young Readers.

Hughes, Langston. (1994). Dream keeper. Scholastic, Inc.

Prelutsky, Jack. (1983). The Random House Book of Poetry for Children. Random House.

Schenk, Beatrice. (1988). Sing a Song of Popcorn. Scholastic Inc.

Silverstein, Shel. (1981). A Light in the Attic. Harper Collins Publishers.

CHAPTER 6:
BLACK HISTORY LESSON PLANS

The purpose of this unit is to expose students to the lives of Black Americans who have made great contributions to our society. The focus of this study will be unsung or unknown blacks that have impacted our world through literature, music, science and government.

Students will be studying the lives and contributions of Black Americans like Frederick Jones, Thomas Dorsey, Alex Haley and the Little Rock Nine. The lessons in this section cover approximately two to four weeks.

BLACK HISTORY LESSON PLANS

FOCUS: Uses the writing process

GEORGIA MIDDLE SCHOOL QCC: 6-23, 50, 69, 7-22, 46, 64, 8-22, 46, 64

AMOUNT OF TIME: 60 minutes

MATERIALS: journals, copies of "Who Am I" activity sheet, and copies of *A Man with a Million Ideas*

INTRODUCTION: Begin the lesson by displaying pictures of famous Black Americans. Call on volunteers to identify the people in the pictures and their contribution(s) to society. Explain that there are many unknown Black Americans who have influenced the growth of our nation.

1. Brainstorm and write in journal what life would be like with only a fourth grade education.

2. Have students complete "Who Am I" activity sheet and discuss their responses.

3. Discuss the term *genre*, and introduce the biography. Allow students to share titles of biographies they have read.

4. Introduce *A Man with a Million Ideas*. Put students in groups of four and assign the following roles.

   - Reader—reads chapter 1 to the group.
   - Recorder—records the questions for the group.
   - Checker—stops the group during reading and ask questions.
   - Presenter—reads group's questions to the class and calls on volunteers to answer the questions.

Each group will read orally chapter 1 of the biography, discuss the chapter and write three summary questions (one knowledge question, one comprehension question, and one critical thinking question).

CLOSURE: Close the lesson by having each group ask their questions to the class. Call on volunteers to predict what will happen in the next chapter.

REFLECTION: _____

_____

_____

_____

_____

WHO AM I?

I received only a fourth grade _____. I taught myself to _____ because I wanted to learn more about building things. I invented a refrigeration unit for transport _____ in 1938.

These units are manufactured today in plants all over the world. The name of the company that makes the refrigeration unit is _____ _____.

There is only one of these plants in Georgia, and it is located in the city of _____. This city was also Georgia's first permanent capital in the late 1800's.

I am credited with over 100 _____. I loved to _____ things, but I was never interested in making _____. I died of _____ cancer in 1961.

BLACK HISTORY LESSON PLANS

FOCUS: Recognizes persuasion techniques in propaganda and advertising

GEORGIA MIDDLE SCHOOL QCC: 6-45, 7-42, 8-43

AMOUNT OF TIME: 60 minutes

MATERIALS: video—taped commercials, transparency of propaganda techniques

INTRODUCTION: Show video- taped commercials. Use transparency to explain each type of commercial.

1. Display transparency with quote about reading by Frederick Jones. Have students read it silently, and then have a volunteer read it orally.

2. Discuss Jones' feelings about reading, and have students brainstorm orally why reading is important. List their responses on the overhead.

3. Group Activity: Divide the class into five groups. Assign each group a propaganda technique, and have them write a commercial in which they persuade people to read. Go over rubric with students.

4. Give each group time to plan and practice their commercials (at least two days).

5. Videotape each commercial and play it for the class. Ask students to identify each group's propaganda technique.

CLOSURE: Have students tell about their favorite commercials and identify the propaganda technique used in the commercial.

REFLECTION: _____
_____
_____
_____
_____

PROPAGANDA TECHNIQUES

****

BANDWAGON

****

1) Mom, all the kids are wearing Arizona jeans.

2) Most professionals use America On Line to surf the net.

****

TESTIMONAL

****

1) Hi, I'm Grant Hill, And I love to eat McDonald's fries during my breaks. Have you had your break today?

2) I'm Halle Berry. I put in some long hours as an actress, so I drink Maxwell House to keep me going.

PROPAGANDA TECHNIQUES

****
EMOTIONAL
****

1) Starburst candy makes your mouth water with its burst of flavor.

2) Try Sprite! A clear, cool and refreshing drink.

****
TRANSFER
****

1) Here are just a few NBA players who donate their money and time to the Boys Club:
Michael Jordan
Shaquille O'Neal
Coby Bryant

2) Wear Elizabeth Taylor's White Diamond and smell like a million bucks.

****
REPETITION
****

Have a coke and a smile.
Coke is sure to make you smile.

Snickers satisfies you.
Satisfy your hunger with snickers.

"You have to read. Find out what others know. You don't have to buy books. Use libraries! You can educate yourself by reading. All my life has been study and work. That's what I get fun out of."

***** Fred M. Jones *****

From: *Man with a Million Ideas*
Author: Virginia Ott & Gloria Swanson

Kimberly Rena Sheffield-Gibbons

RUBRIC FOR COMMERCIALS

NAME: _____ DATE: _____

DIRECTIONS: Read each section below, and circle a number from 0—10.
O is poor and 10 is excellent.

1. Did the group present a jingle or slogan?   1 2 3 4 5 6 7 8 9 10

2. Did the group use props in the commercial?   1 2 3 4 5 6 7 8 9 10

3. Did the group present the commercial in a way   1 2 3 4 5 6 7 8 9 10
   so that the propaganda technique could be easily
   identified?

4. Did all group members participate?   1 2 3 4 5 6 7 8 9 10

5. Did group members work cooperatively?   1 2 3 4 5 6 7 8 9 10

6. Did actors speak clearly and loudly?   1 2 3 4 5 6 7 8 9 10

7. Was the commercial persuasive?   1 2 3 4 5 6 7 8 9 10

8. Was the commercial creative?   1 2 3 4 5 6 7 8 9 10

9. Was the propaganda technique used suitable   1 2 3 4 5 6 7 8 9 10
   for this commercial?

10. Overall Performance   1 2 3 4 5 6 7 8 9 10

Total Score/Comments: _____
_____
_____
_____
_____

BLACK HISTORY LESSON PLANS

FOCUS: Participates in oral presentations

GEORGIA MIDDLE SCHOOL QCC: 6-62—65, 7-57—60, 8-57 - 60

AMOUNT OF TIME: 60 minutes

MATERIALS: *Precious Lord and other Songs* by Thomas Dorsey, tape player, lyrics of Dorsey's music, "Snip-it" activity sheet, Dorsey biographical transparency

INTRODUCTION: Begin the lesson by playing the music of Thomas Dorsey. Play the entire cassette.

1. Play snip-its of a few songs and have students complete the "Snip-its" activity sheet.

2. Put the Dorsey biographical transparency on the overhead and have students read it silently. Then have a student read it orally.

3. Remove the transparency and have students list all they can remember from the selection.

4. Have students reread the transparency and add or make corrections to their lists.

5. Divide the class into three different groups. Each group will select a Dorsey song and practice performing it in one of the following ways: singing, choral reading, or dramatization.

6. After ample practice time, allow each group to perform.

CLOSURE: Have one group write letters to the Thomas Dorsey Foundation requesting additional information and/or asking questions. Another group can draw pictures of Dorsey, and the other group can write poems about the gospel musician. Mail to:

The Thomas Dorsey Foundation
571 W. Highway 78
Villa Rica, GA 30180

REFLECTION: _____
_____
_____
_____
_____

SNIP-IT ACTIVITY SHEET

DIRECTIONS: Your teacher will play snip-its of a few songs. Listen to the music and answer each question below. (20pts. each)

1. What is the title of the first song?

2. Why did Thomas Dorsey write this song?

3. How does the speaker feel in the second song?

4. Name one word that is repeated in the second song.

5. What is the last song about?

THOMAS DORSEY

Born in Villa Rica, Georgia in 1899, Thomas A. Dorsey had an interest in music at an early age. He said that he walked four miles a day (four days of the week) to piano lessons. Dorsey began playing blues after studying at a music college in Chicago. Thomas played blues piano in clubs throughout Chicago.

After attending a Baptist Convention in Chicago and hearing a spiritual song, Thomas devoted himself to gospel songs. *Take My Hand Precious Lord* is one of the most popular gospel songs. It was written after the death of his wife and child.

Dorsey's songs are sung all over the country by many choirs, soloists, and celebrities. Mahalia Jackson and Elvis Presley sang Dorsey's gospels in concerts.

By the time of his death in 1993, Thomas Dorsey had written over 1,000 gospel songs. People come from far and near to pay tribute to Dorsey. The Thomas Dorsey Foundation hosts a festival each Spring in Dorsey's birthplace of Villa Rica, Georgia. Gospel artists and blues musicians come share their talents and entertain the crowds. The festival is held each June, and is an all day event.

BLACK HISTORY LESSON PLANS

FOCUS: Uses a research process

GEORGIA MIDDLE SCHOOL QCC: 6-52, 53, 7-49, 50, 8-46, 49

AMOUNT OF TIME: 60 minutes

MATERIALS: novels by Alex Haley, picture of Haley, biographical information on Alex Haley, Family Tree Transparency

INTRODUCTION: Have Haley's books and picture on display. Share biographical information.

1. Discuss Haley's research and the completion of *Roots*.

2. Read excerpts from *Roots* to the class, and have students write a response in their journal.

3. Then show segments of the movie that coincide with the excerpts.

4. Compare and contrast the book and the movie.

5. Model for students how to do a family tree.

6. Let students fill in as much as they can on their family tree, and give them a few days to complete it at home. Encourage students to go to the public library and/or courthouse to locate family history.

CLOSURE: Share family traditions/special stories.

REFLECTION: _____
_____
_____
_____
_____

MY FAMILY TREE

My Name: _____ **Date of Birth:** _____

My Siblings: _____

_____

My Mother	My Father
Mother's Siblings	**Father's Siblings**
Mother's Parents	**Father's Parents**
Grandpa's Siblings	**Grandpa's Siblings**

Grandma's Siblings	**Grandma's Siblings**
Grandpa's Parents	**Grandpa's Parents**
Grandma's Parents	**Grandma's Parents**

BLACK HISTORY LESSON PLANS

FOCUS: Describes cultures and values presented in literature

GEORGIA MIDDLE SCHOOL QCC: 6-28, 29, 7-27, 28, 8-27, 28

AMOUNT OF TIME: 60 minutes

MATERIALS: video clips of the Little Rock Nine school integration, a copy of *Freedom's Children* edited by Ellen Levine, Avon Books and anticipation guide activity sheet

INTRODUCTION: Show video clips of the Little Rock Nine.

1. Have students complete the anticipation guide, and then discuss it.

2. Read excerpts from *Freedom's Children* and discuss.

3. Imagine you are one of the students integrating a school in the 60's. Write a reflection in your journal.

4. Have student pairs research information on Brown vs. Board of Education using the internet.

CLOSURE: Discuss roles of people in the judicial system (attorney, judge, court reporter, etc.).

- Plan ahead and invite local courthouse representatives to speak to the class.
- Have students prepare questions to ask the guests.
- Take a field trip to the courthouse. Get a guided tour and sit in on a court case.

REFLECTION: _____

_____

_____

_____

_____

ANTICIPATION GUIDE

DIRECTIONS: Read the statements below. Write <u>A</u> on the blank if you agree with the statement. Write <u>D</u> on the blank if you disagree with the statement.

1. _____   All people are equal.

2. _____   Students should be able to go to school anywhere.

3. _____   Schools are responsible for making sure students are safe.

4. _____   Teachers should be willing to help all students.

BLACK HISTORY LESSON PLANS

FOCUS: Describes cultures and values presented in literature

GEORGIA MIDDLE SCHOOL QCC: 6-26,30, 7-25, 29, 8-25, 29

AMOUNT OF TIME: 60 minutes (at least 2 days)

MATERIALS: video clips of courtroom scenes, transcript of Brown vs. Board of Education, courtroom props

INTRODUCTION: Show video clips of courtroom scenes. Stop the video every few minutes and have students respond.

1. Discuss the roles of participants in the video.

2. Have students braistorm ideas for a class courtroom scene based on Brown vs. Board of Education.

3. Discuss the role of each participant in the Brown vs. Board of Education case (emotions, responsibilities, pressures, etc.).

4. Let students plan and perform a mock trial. Video their performance.

CLOSURE: Let students share what they learned from their internet research of Brown vs. Board of Education, and discuss the transcript.

REFLECTION: _____
_____
_____
_____
_____

BLACK HISTORY PROJECTS

❑ Black History Quiz Bowl—Let students do the research and come up with the questions. Make copies of the questions for students to study. Let them find the answers, but be sure to go over the questions and answers before the bowl. Divide the class into two teams and ask questions. Award the team with the most points.

❑ Black History Fair—Just like the Science Fair except students create a display of Black Americans and their contributions. Make it a school wide project, and invite parents and the community.

❑ Student/Parent Literary Contest—Encourage parents and students to work together researching a Black American, and share their findings through character portrayals, dramatizations, poetry readings, etc. Invite business partners to judge the event.

❑ Black History Booklet—Put together a biographical sketch of Black Americans. Include pictures, poems, quotes, etc.

❑ Diorama—Students can create a display that depicts the life of a Black American they learned about during the unit.

BLACK HISTORY RESOURCES

POETRY

Adoff, Arnold. *The Poetry of Black America: Anthology of the 20ᵗʰ Century.* This anthology includes over three hundred poems by black poets.

Bontemps, Arna, compiler. *Anthology of African American Poetry for Young People.* This is a cassette tape of poems by various Black Americans.

Brooks, Gwendolyn. *BronzevilleBoys and Girls.* This book explores children and their feelings.

Byran, Ashley. *I'm Going to Sing: Black American Spirituals.* This text includes musical arrangements.

Greenfield, Eloise. *Under the Sunday Tree.* Poems explore life in the Bahamas.

Hughes, Langston. *The Dream Keeper.* This is a collection of poems that focus on black heritage.

Silverstein, Shel. A Light in the Attic. This is a collection of humorous poems.

FICTION

Bryan, Ashley. *Turtle Knows Your Name.* This folktale is from the West Indies.

Campbell, Barbara. *A Girl Called Bob and a Horse Called Yoki.* An eight-year old girl saves a horse from the glue factory.

Hamilton, Virginia. *The Bells of Christmas.* This is the story of a prosperous black family's Christmas experiences during the 1890's.

Hamilton, Virginia.*The House of Dies Drear.* This is a suspense story about a family living in a home that was a station of the Underground Railroad.

Lester, Julius. *How Many Spots Does a Leopard Have?* Folktales in this collection reflect both African and Jewish traditions.

Myers, Walter Dean. *Scorpions.* A boy faces problems with a gang.

Taylor, Mildred. *The Gold Cadillac.* A black family experiences racial prejudice when they try to drive an expensive car to the segregated South.

BIOGRAPHIES

Adoff, Arnold. *Malcolm X.* This is a biography for young readers.

Davis, Ossie. *Langston: A Play.* Scenes from Hughe's life are presented in play format.

DeKay, James T. *Meet Martin Luther King, Jr.* This biography stresses the magnitude of M.L.K.'s work and the reasons he fought against injustice.

Ferris, Jeri. *Go Free or Die: A Story of Harriet Tubman.* This biography describes Tubman's experiences during slavery and the Underground Railroad.

Greenfield, Eloise. *Paul Robeson.* This book highlights the achievements and struggles of an artist and leader.

Greenfield, Eloise. *Rosa Parks.* This is the story of a woman who refused to give up her seat on the bus.

Hamilton, Virginia. *Anthony Burns: The Defeat and Triumph of a Fugitive Slave.* This is the story of the escaped slave whose trial caused riots in Boston.

Miller, Douglas. *Frederick Douglass and the Fight for Freedom.* This book tells the life of an escaped slave turned abolitionist.

Patterson, Lillie. *Sure Hands, Strong Heart: The Life of Daniel Hale Williams.* This is a biography of a black physician who worked for interracial hospitals.

Potter, Joan & Claytor, Constance. *African-American Firsts: Famous, Little-Known and Unsung Triumphs of Blacks in America*. This is a great resource to use for trivia questions.

Riley, Dorothy Winbush. *My Soul Looks Back, 'Less I Forget: A Collection of Quotations by People of Color*. This book has numerous quotes on a varitey of topics and is a good resource for student speeches and presentations.

CHAPTER 7:
RUBRICS

Grading can be a very tedious chore for teachers. This chapter offers alternative ways to assess student learning. Rubrics, and progress charts can be very helpful in determining student scores. Evaluations are also beneficial because they give students and teachers an opportunity to reflect and respond to lessons. The assessment tools in this section are very practical, and they clearly define student expectations.

WRITING RUBRIC

NAME: _____ GRADE: _____ DATE: _____

Type of Writing:	How to Paragraph	Comparison/Contrast	Cause/Effect	Narrative
(circle one)	Descriptive	Persuasive	Poetry	Creative

DIRECTIONS: Using the criteria below, rate each writing.

CONTENT (75%)
1. The writing begins with a clear topic sentence. (5 pts.) _____
2. The writing has at least three detail sentences that support the topic. (15 pts.) _____
3. The writing is well-planned and thought out. (10 pts.) _____
4. The writing has a clear closing sentence. (5 pts.) _____
5. The writer stays on the topic. (10 pts.) _____
6. The writer has a sense of his/her audience. (5 pts.) _____
7. The writer uses a variety of different kinds of sentences. (10 pts.) _____
8. Overall, the writing is appropriate and makes sense. (15 pts.) _____

MECHANICS (25%)
9. Sentences and words are capitalized correctly. (5 pts.) _____
10. Sentences and words are punctuated correctly. (5 pts.) _____
11. Sentences have few spelling errors (less than 5). (5 pts.) _____
12. Subjects and verbs agee in all sentences. (5 pts.) _____
13. Overall, writing is neat and readable. (5 pts.) _____

TOTAL _____

WRITING STRENGTHS/WEAKNESSES: _____
_____
_____

WRITING STRATEGIES: _____
_____
_____

ORAL READING RUBRIC

NAME: _____ GRADE: _____ DATE: _____

TITLE OF READING SELECTION: _____

GENRE: AUTOBIOGRAPHY   BIOGRAPHY   DRAMA   ESSAY
(circle one)   FOLKTALE   MYTH   POETRY   SHORT STORY

DIRECTIONS: Read each statement below, and rate the reader on a scale of 0—
        10 by circling a number. Zero is poor and ten is excellent.

FLUENCY
1. The reader has good volume.   1 2 3 4 5 6 7 8 9 10
2. The reader has a good pace.   1 2 3 4 5 6 7 8 9 10
3. The reader enunciates clearly.   1 2 3 4 5 6 7 8 9 10
4. The reader uses expression.   1 2 3 4 5 6 7 8 9 10
5. The reader self-corrects when he/she makes
    a mistake.   1 2 3 4 5 6 7 8 9 10

COMPREHENSION
6. The reader uses context clues to figure out
    unknown words.   1 2 3 4 5 6 7 8 9 10
7. The reader can decode unknown words.   1 2 3 4 5 6 7 8 9 10
8. The reader can answer questions about what
    he/she is reading.   1 2 3 4 5 6 7 8 9 10
9. The reader can summarize what he/she is
    reading.   1 2 3 4 5 6 7 8 9 10
10. The reader makes predictions.   1 2 3 4 5 6 7 8 9 10
11. The reader draws conclusions.   1 2 3 4 5 6 7 8 9 10

TOTAL POINTS   _____

READING ERRORS (check all that apply)
❑ Rereads a word or phrase.   _____
❑ Leaves out a word or phrase.   _____
❑ Replaces a word or phrase for another.   _____

116

❑ Hesitant about attacking unknown words. _____
❑ Pauses unnecessarily. _____
❑ Doesn't pause or stop for punctuation. _____
❑ Skips a line. _____

STRATEGIES: _____

_____

_____

_____

_____

Kimberly Rena Sheffield-Gibbons

RUBRIC FOR ORAL PRESENTATIONS

NAME: _____ GRADE: _____ DATE: _____

TYPE OF PRESENTATION: CHORAL READING   SPEECH   POETRY RECITAL
(circle one)   STORY TELLING

DIRECTIONS: Read each statement and give a point from 1—10. One is low
              and ten is high.

CONTENT (5pts. each)
1. The speech began in a way to catch the audience's attention. _____
2. The speech was clear and easy to follow. _____
3. The speech was interesting. _____
4. The speech was appropriate for the audience. _____

DELIVERY (10pts. each)
5. The speaker spoke loudly and clearly. _____
6. The speaker used appropriate grammar. _____
7. The speaker was knowledgeable of the subject. _____
8. The speaker was confident and enthusiastic. _____
9. The speaker's voice expression and facial expressions were
   appropriate. _____
10. The speaker used appropriate body language and gestures. _____

VISUAL AIDS (5pts. each)
11. The speaker used at least one visual (chart, board, poster,
    slide show, etc.). _____
12. The speaker was comfortable using visual. _____
13. Visuals were appropriate for audience. _____
14. Visuals were neat and readable. _____

TOTAL _____

COMMENTS: _____
_____
_____
_____
_____

RUBRIC FOR DRAMATIC PRESENTATIONS

NAME: _____ GRADE: _____ DATE: _____

TYPE OF DRAMA: ROLE PLAYING   SKIT   PLAY
(circle one)   CHARACTER PORTRAYAL

DIRECTIONS: Each statement below is worth ten points. Rate each statement from 0—10.

STAGE PRESENCE
- The student actor was calm and confident. _____
- The student actor made the character believable. _____
- The student actor wore an appropriate costume(s). _____
- The student actor enunciated well. _____
- The student actor spoke loud enough. _____
- The student actor used expression. _____
- The student actor followed stage directions. _____

PREPARATION
- The student actor practiced in class alone/with other student actors. _____
- The student worked cooperatively with other cast members. _____
- The student actor memorized his/her lines. _____

TOTAL _____

YOU DID A GOOD JOB: _____
_____
_____
_____

PLEASE WORK ON: _____
_____
_____
_____

Kimberly Rena Sheffield-Gibbons

PROGRESS CHART

NAME: _____ BIRTHDATE: _____ GRADE: _____

PARENT(S): _____ TELEPHONE #: _____

ADDRESS: _____
_____

DIRECTIONS: Use this chart throughout the year to monitor each student's
academic and behavioral progress. Be sure to date each entry.

TEACHER OBSERVATIONS (1ST Week of School)): _____
_____
_____
_____

INTERVENTIONS (If applicable): _____
_____
_____

TEACHER OBSERVATIONS (1ST Month of School): _____
_____
_____
_____

INTERVENTIONS (If applicable): _____
_____
_____

TEACHER OBSERVATIONS (1ST Grading Period): _____
_____
_____
_____

INTERVENTIONS (If applicable): _____
_____
_____

TEACHER OBSERVATIONS (1ST Semester): _____

_____

_____

_____

INTERVENTIONS (If applicable): _____

_____

_____

TEACHER OBSERVATIONS (Midyear): _____

_____

_____

_____

INTERVENTIONS (If applicable): _____

_____

_____

TEACHER OBSERVATIONS (End of Year): _____

_____

_____

_____

RECOMMENDATIONS: _____

_____

_____

_____

STATE TEST SCORE: _____   **STATE TEST SCORE:** _____
(previous year)   (current year)

POINTS GAINED: _____   **POINTS LOST:** _____

TEST STRENGTHS:

_____

_____

TEST WEAKNESSES:

_____

_____

Teacher Signature: _____ Date: _____

PROGRESS CHART

Use this chart to monitor your teaching throughout the year. Be honest with yourself. Make improvements when needed. Reward yourself when you exceed your expectations.

DIRECTIONS: Make several copies of this chart. At different intervals during the year, find time to rate your teaching using the scale below.

- Above and beyond =   5
- Excellent =   4
- Good =   3
- Average =   2
- Poor =   1

PLANNING

1) I spend at least one hour each week thinking through and planning lessons.   1 2 3 4 5
2) I plan lessons that make learning fun for students even if I have to spend more time planning, or even if I have to spend money.   1 2 3 4 5
3) I plan lessons that provide me an opportunity to spend time with each student one-on-one.   1 2 3 4 5
4) I read through material (textbook, handouts, etc.) before I present it to students.   1 2 3 4 5
5) Besides the textbook, I use additional resources.   1 2 3 4 5
6) I attend workshops, conferences, and take courses, so I can keep learning.   1 2 3 4 5

INSTRUCTION

7) I model the skills I want students to learn.   1 2 3 4 5
8) I show expression and enthusiasm when presenting lessons.   1 2 3 4 5
9) I teach lessons each day to appeal to students' learning styles.   1 2 3 4 5
10) I try a variety of teaching methods.   1 2 3 4 5
11) I encourage and praise students.   1 2 3 4 5

BEHAVIOR

12) I allow students to voice their opinion as long as they do so appropriately.   1 2 3 4 5

122

13) I often ask for student input regarding lessons.   1 2 3 4 5
14) I listen to my students.   1 2 3 4 5
15) I give each student a fresh start each day.   1 2 3 4 5
16) I am patient with students and try to see their needs. 1 2 3 4 5
17) I discipline all students fairly regardless of race, social
    status, etc.   1 2 3 4 5
18) I am firm, yet polite to my students.   1 2 3 4 5

PARENT CONTACT
19) I make contact with parents each grading period. (note,
    phone call, conference)   1 2 3 4 5
20) I am honest with parents about their child's behavior and
    academic progress.   1 2 3 4 5

TOTAL   _____

SCORE INTEPRETATION:

100—99 =   You are a superior teacher. You always go that extra mile to meet your students' needs.

You students really love and respect you, and your colleagues praise and admire you.

You are willing to try new things even though it may be challenging.

You may not always receive the recognition you deserve, but your rewards are many.

89—80 =   You are a very good teacher, and you enjoy working with students.

You work very hard and are well-liked by your students and peers.

You plan fun lessons for students, but not as often as you should.

79—70 =   You are an average teacher. You go strictly by the book and never challenge the students.

You probably use the same lesson plans year after year.

You need to spend time reflecting and decide if this is a profession you want to continue.

69 - below =   You do not enjoy teaching at all. Your students probably do a lot of seat work.
You were probably an excellent teacher at one time, but now you are burned out.
Think about your students and choose another path.

REFLECTIONS: _____

_____
_____
_____

THINGS TO TRY:

1.

2.

3.

4.

5.

EVALUATION

DIRECTIONS: Read each statement and evaluate the lesson. Please give your honest opinion, and do not write your name on this sheet.

- Strongly Agree = 5
- Agree = 4
- Undecided = 3
- Strongly Disagree = 2
- Disagree = 1

1) The lesson was well planned and organized.   1 2 3 4 5

2) The lesson was interesting and fun.   1 2 3 4 5

3) The lesson was presented so I could understand.   1 2 3 4 5

4) The teacher spoke loudly and clearly.   1 2 3 4 5

5) The teacher did a good job presenting the lesson.   1 2 3 4 5

6) The teacher involved the students in the lesson.   1 2 3 4 5

7) The teacher used visual aids to present the lesson.   1 2 3 4 5

8) The teacher was excited about the lesson and motivated me.   1 2 3 4 5

9) The teacher should repeat this lesson with other students.   1 2 3 4 5

10) Overall, this was a very enjoyable learning experience.   1 2 3 4 5

- What did you like most about this lesson?

- What did you like least about this lesson?

EVALUATION

DIRECTIONS: Teachers, this is an evaluation for you. Reflect on the lesson, and give your honest opinion.

- Strongly Agree =   5
- Agree =   4
- Undecided =   3
- Strongly Disagree =   2
- Disagree =   1

1) The lesson opener caught students' attention.   1 2 3 4 5

2) The lesson content was appropriate for my students.   1 2 3 4 5

3) The lesson was both student centered and teacher centered.   1 2 3 4 5

4) The lesson ended appropriately.   1 2 3 4 5

5) The lesson made students think.   1 2 3 4 5

6) I kept students focused and on task.   1 2 3 4 5

7) I used time wisely.   1 2 3 4 5

8) I had all materials and equipment set up and ready.   1 2 3 4 5

9) I enjoyed teaching the lesson.   1 2 3 4 5

10) I would teach this lesson again.   1 2 3 4 5

REFLECTION: Think about what worked well in this lesson and any improvements you would make.

_____

_____

_____

BOOK EVALUATION

Teachers, please take a few minutes and give your opinion of *The Teacher's Right Hand*. Rate each statement according to the scale below.

- 4 = Excellent
- 3 = Good
- 2 = Average
- 1 = Poor
- N/A = Not applicable (not known)

STRATEGIES

1) Strategies are well written and easy to follow.   1 2 3 4 N/A

2) Strategies are practical and very helpful.   1 2 3 4 N/A

3) After trying these strategies, I saw positive results with students.   1 2 3 4 N/A

LESSON PLANS

4) The lesson plans were creative and original.   1 2 3 4 N/A

5) The lesson plans were high interest.   1 2 3 4 N/A

6) The activities correlated with the objectives well.   1 2 3 4 N/A

7) The lesson plans included a variety of objectives.   1 2 3 4 N/A

ASSESSMENT

8) The assessment tools were practical and easy to follow.   1 2 3 4 N/A

9) Each assessment addressed important skills.   1 2 3 4 N/A

10) Assessments clearly defined student expectations.   1 2 3 4 N/A

COMMENTS: _____

_____

_____

_____

Please mail your evaluation to
Kimberly S. Gibbons
7184 Pinetucky Road
Wadley, GA 30477

CHAPTER 8:

INSPIRATIONAL POEMS

I began writing poetry as a college student. I wrote as a way to express my feelings to others. I was very shy growing up, and it was hard for me to tell others how I felt. The first poems I wrote were about friendship. I also wrote poems about God and my relationship with Him.

Some of the poems were written to honor people who have touched my life, and some were requests I wrote for other people. The poems you are about to read are my originals. I hope you will find them humorous, inspiring and uplifting.

A CLASSROOM SOMEWHERE

"Johnny, where is your textbook?" the teacher shouts.
"Boy, if you don't have that book tomorrow, you and I are gonna have it out!
You need your text. You can't learn any other way.
That's why you are required to bring it everyday.
This book is like the Bible. You must read it to learn.
Then, when I ask questions, all A's you're sure to earn."

"Look on with Nathan so you won't daydream and stare,
And Johnny, try to stay focused and aware.
This is an important topic, and the text explains it so well.
If you follow along, you can finish reading before the ring of the bell.
We will discuss the chapter after you read.
Then you may ask questions, if you need."

Tonight for homework write a summary of the chapter.
You will discuss it in groups and take a quiz after.
So read carefully, class and study hard tonight.
You shouldn't have any problems with the summary you write.

** Kimberly S. Gibbons: February 12, 1997 **

A MODEL STUDENT
(IN MEMORY OF LETESHIA NELSON)
(AUGUST 29, 1983—AUGUST 29, 1998)

Every once in a while, a student comes along who meets the teacher's
expectations and goals,
Leteshia Nelson was one of those.
She was so calm, quiet and polite.
She was an honor roll student, very bright.
Leteshia had such a beautiful smile that would brighten anyone's day,
And she always had nothing but pleasant words to say.

Leteshia Nelson was a model student in my classroom.
She followed the rules,
And she used her own tools.
She got along well with her peers
Always there for others, with a listening ear.
She was attentive and on task,
And if she didn't understand, many questions she'd ask.

It was a joy and a pleasure to teach
Such a model student so easy to reach.
Leteshia, like me, loved for things to be in order and neat.
She often stayed after school to dust my room and straighten every seat.
She said to me many times, "Mrs. Gibbons, let me come clean up your house,
sometime."
I would quickly say, "Leteshia, nobody wants to clean up a house of mine."

Proverbs 22:6 says, "Train up a child in the way he should go; and when
he is old, he will not depart."
It was obvious that Leteshia was trained in the Lord because she had such
a big heart.
She had a sweet spirit and so much love
That couldn't have come from anyone else but God above.

I'm proud to have taught Leteshia.
I'm glad the Lord let our paths cross,
For she was such a blessing to me.
She helped me a better teacher, be.
When a student like Leteshia comes through your classroom door,
You can't help but to give a little bit more.
Family and friends, Leteshia will be missed, but don't be alarmed,
For she has taken her rest in the safety of God's arms.

** Kimberly S. Gibbons: September 5, 1998 **

A NEW SCHOOL YEAR

As a new school year takes place,
There are many challenges teachers face.
To help children learn in so many ways
In a short amount of time, 190 days.
Academics is not the only thing sought,
But there are many life lessons taught.

There are moments when I don't reach
Some of the students I am trying to teach.
I don't give up, but I reflect and pray.
Then try again another day.
I start each day with patience and love
Because teaching is my calling from God above.

** Kimberly S. Gibbons: September 1, 1998 **

A TEACHER IS LIKE A PROPHET

A teacher, like a prophet has a divine calling.
She has been appointed by God to keep children from falling.
To keep students from falling, a teacher must be a friend,
For a listening ear is what helps a broken heart to mend.
A teacher should be respectful and kind
If she wants her students to listen and mind.
Teachers must be careful what they say and do.
They not only teach, but they are role models, too.
All of these characteristics are representative of a prophet,
one who is chosen and set aside.
Likewise, a teacher is commissioned as a guide.
To guide students intellectually, physically, emotionally and
spiritually,
So they can begin to see the world realistically.

Like a prophet, a teacher has a special message to deliver.
Some students listen and take heed,
And others feel there is just no need.
Still the teacher must impart knowledge and information
Because God has called her to help shape the nation.
Like a prophet, a teacher doesn't quit when the message
falls on a deaf ear.
Instead, she whispers to God, "Help me to make it through this
school year."
Just as the bible prophets of old
A teacher has to be quite bold.
For she never knows what kind of child will enter her classroom.
A child's who hungry and cold
One who will not listen to what he's told.
A student who has no personal hygiene,
Or one who has to wear the same old blue jeans.
A child who has no home
One who cuts class just to roam.

A student who comes to school late,
Or one who doesn't know his birthdate.
A child who is strung out on drugs
One who's goal in life is to be a thug.
A student who doesn't give a damn and will tell you so,
Or a promiscuous girl who just can't say no.
A prophet doesn't always know what kind of people he will face.
Yet he does his job because he has God's protection and grace.
Like a prophet, a teacher goes prepared and ready for the class.
For she must know the material before presenting it to the class.

A teacher neither a prophet's labors are in vain.
For there are many rewards to be gained.
To see just one make a change for the better
Is worth all the time and effort spent.
No amount of money can top that.
So teachers hold to your prophecy
Keep encouraging, praising and loving children.
Continue to be a friend, a mother, a father, a nurse, a counselor, or
whatever else it takes.
Soon there will be no more broken hearts to mend
Because your service to children will one day end.
Continue to be patient, for your retirement day is coming soon.
God is preparing you a special room.
He wants this room to be the very best
Before He takes you into His kingdom to rest.

** Kimberly S. Gibbons: May 28, 1997 **

Kimberly Rena Sheffield-Gibbons

AN INSPIRING PROFESSOR
(DEDICATED TO DR. ELAINE ROBERTS @ STATE UNIVERSITY OF WEST GEORGIA)

Dr. Roberts, you have been such an inspiration to me.
Your encouraging words have really uplifted me.
I'm glad I enrolled in your class session
Because I was about to quit the teaching profession.
I was very burned out and had lost hope,
But your lectures motivated me, and now I want to continue to teach,
For there are so many young people to reach.
As a teacher, I have an important role,
And that is to help students achieve their goals.

You have a very optimistic view of education.
"Things in education will get better," you'd often say.
"Teachers must be patient, for change is on the way."
"We can't give up on kids no matter what their age."
"We must try many strategies to keep them engaged."
"It's never too late," you'd often say.
"All students can be helped in some way."

Dr. Roberts, thanks for your encouraging words.
Thanks for the many lesson ideas.
Thanks for your enthusiasm and concern.
Thanks for your confidence in me.
My transition from classroom teacher to fulltime graduate student
was very pleasant thanks to you.
I'll always remember you and the many lessons I learned, too.
The reading courses were a great help and gave me many ideas.
I'm more motivated to help students improve their reading skills.
Professor Roberts, I'll never forget how you touched my life and
in so many ways inspired me.
Keep doing great things at the University.

** Kimberly S. Gibbons: June 18, 1997 **

FROM JOHNNY TO HIS TEACHER

Teacher, I left my book at home on my bed.
I can't get all that stuff inside my head.
Why do we always use that book?
We can learn from other sources if you'd let us look.
The textbook scares me, and I don't understand it.
Maybe if you taught it bit by bit,
I could get just a little grasp of it.

Teacher, I don't think Nathan has a clue.
He's always asking me what to do.
Even after this chapter I've read,
I don't think I can tell you what it said.
How will I be able to answer questions?
How can I write a summary?
How can I make sense of this?
I just don't know what to do.
Teacher, is there anyway I could get help from you?

Teacher, please show me what I'm doing wrong.
So I can learn to read this textbook on my own.
Show me how to take notes and write.
Then, I will be able to do my homework at night.
Teacher, I'm not asking to be your buddy.
I just want to learn how to study.

** Kimberly S. Gibbons: February 12, 1997 **

FROM STUDENT TO TEACHER
(DEDICATED TO MY FIRST SUNDAY SCHOOL TEACHER: MRS. ANN TAYLOR)

"Be careful what you say and do."
Those words were often quoted by you.
"You may be the only Bible some people read," you'd go on to say.
As my Sunday school teacher, you were sharing with your students
about living the Christian Way.

As a teen, I didn't quite understand those words,
But through your persistent teaching, I heard.
Eventually I came to understand, "Be careful what you say and do."
I find myself quoting those same words, too.

As a Christian, I must be careful what I say and do.
As an educator, I must be careful what I say and do.
As a youth leader, I must be careful what I say and do.
And as a wife, I must be careful what I say and do.

I'm proud to say I'm a student you reached,
And I'm so glad you were persistent, Teach.
You caught my attention through your innovative way.
One lesson you used a JC Penney catalog, do you remember that day?

You passed it around and asked each student to find his favorite place.
Without hesitation, each of us found our special place.
There was a very concerned look on your face.
You said, "Now can any of you find Matthew, Mark, Luke or John?
They all tell the story of God's Only Son."

The lesson you taught that day about studying God's Word
That one, too didn't go unheard.
Your teaching has touched my life in so many ways.
I'm grateful you were my teacher in those earlier days.

Thanks Ann for your examle, your encouragement, and your enthusiasm
while teaching me.
Thanks for the teaching opportunity you gave to me.
Thanks for the knowledge and wisdom you share.
May God forever keep you in His care.

** Kimberly S. Gibbons: September 27, 1996

GO TO THE WORD

Go to the Word in trying times.
Then get on your knees and tell Jesus your mind.
He will hear you if you are sincere.
For He promised to always be near.

Go to the Word when sad and blue.
The Savior will be there to comfort you.
He will give you mercy and grace.
For His love is like none other in the human race.

Go to the Word each and every day.
Let Jesus show you the way.
He invites you to come unto Him
All who are burdened and heavy-ladened,
For He will give you rest.
If you need a burden bearer, Jesus is the best.

Go to the Word, study to show thyself approved,
So in difficullt times you will stand unmoved.
Make yourself ready for Jesus' return,
So a Home on high you can earn.

** Kimberly S. Gibbons: March 26, 1999 **

IT'S GOOD TO KNOW THE LORD"

It's good to know the Lord.
If you don't know Him, come on board.
He is the Way, the Truth and the Life.
He'll help you through those moments of strife.
The Lord will be your refuge, your hiding place.
He'll freely give you His mercy and grace.
If you don't know the Lord ask Him to come in.
He'll rescue you and wipe away your sin.

It's good to know the Lord, for He's the only One
who can save your soul,
And keep you from spending eternity in Hell's fiery hole.
You'll find none other on earth like the Lord,
So why not get to know the Lord.
He'll watch over you day and night.
There is no way to escape from the Lord's sight.
He promises to always be there.
No one else shows such constant care.

It's good to know the Lord because He surrounds you
With His outstretched arm,
And continuously keeps you from hurt and harm.
When you know the Lord, there's no need to worry from day to day
Because blessings will surely come your way.
It's good to know the Lord.
If you don't know Him, come on board.
He'll be back soon to take His "own" through those pearly gates,
So get to know the Lord before it's too late!

** Kimberly S. Gibbons: November 15, 1997 **

LIVE SO GOD CAN USE YOU

Live so God can use you,
Not according to what the world says do.
Talk right—holy and undefiled.
Speak words of wisdom and make God proud.
Walk in a manner that will please.
Then God will hear you when you are on your knees.

Live so God can use you everyday.
Then you can lead others in God's way.
Be careful what you say and do.
Others are always watching you.
Since you might be the only bible some people read,
Always be ready to help those in need.

Live so God can use you, stop playing around,
Or you'll be caught with works undone when the trumpets sound.
Pack up, get ready, Jesus will come in a twinkle
For a church without spot or wrinkle.
Will you be ready, or lost in a stare
When saints are caught up to meet Jesus in the air.

** Kimberly S. Gibbons: April 6, 1999

THE EARTH

The earth is the place I live.
I like it because people are willing to give.
The earth is divided into 4 spheres.
There are 365 days in a year.

There is more water on the earth than land.
Many features make our earth so grand!
We have 7 continents that vary in size.
We can watch the moon, the stars and the sun rise.

The earth has many natural resources for us to use.
We must use them wisely, or we will lose.
The air we breathe, the water we drink, the sun we see
All help us to live abundantly.

There's no place I'd rather be than the earth.
I'm glad I was placed here during my birth.
The earth has so many wonders to behold.
Let's preserve it so it can grow OLD, OLD, OLD.

** Kimberly S. Gibbons: September 18, 1995

THE FUNNY MAN

He is known as the funny man.
He makes people laugh all over the land.
You can see him on the stage.
I bet he earns an awesome wage.

This funny man has a large family.
He often tells jokes about its history.
I like the one about the birth of his first child.
He really had the audience going wild.

He is known as a legendary comic who eases strife.
His jokes poke fun at real life.
This funny man is one you need to see
His name is William (Bill) Cosby.

** Kimberly S. Gibbons: April 24, 1995

THE POWER OF MUSIC

Music is a powerful form of communication.
Music tells the story of our nation.
From Folk songs to Negro spirituals,
Music expresses a culture's many rituals.

The power of music
Its rhythms,
Its lyrics,
Its form,
Its melody,
Its instruments,
All make music so magical, so rich, and so alive, it seems.
Without the power of music, we'd lose our dreams.
We escape to other worlds through music and song.
We cry, we laugh and we sing along.
The power of music, what an impact!
Can you imagine without it, how people would act?

Music shapes our thinking in so many ways,
It guides us through those gloomy days.
Music, music fills the air
Country, R&B and Jazz are heard everywhere.
Pop, Folk, Gospel and Rap
Are other types of music that entrap.

Music catches our attention and alerts the brain
To lead us on a journey down memory lane.
Music make us think of the present and the future, too.
It is a powerful art form we easily connect to.
The power of music,
The power of music,
Imagine our world if we didn't use it.

** Kimberly S. Gibbons: February 6, 1997

USING WHAT YOU HAVE

Use what you have—bring out your ability.
Then success will not just be a possibility.
Rely on your own skills to get you through.
You will be amazed at what you can do.
Stop trying to be someone else.
Be yourself, go ahead and make that step.

Use what you have—some say use what you got.
How will you ever know whether you can do it or not.
Be like the little engine who said, "I know I can."
Don't be afraid to take a stand.
Be among the few and the proud.
Those who have confidence in self and not doubt.

Use what you have that's what God requires of you.
Using what you have and giving your best to what you do.
For if you don't use your own tools,
You are the one who will lose.
Don't wait and regret the road you didn't take.
Use what you have before it's too late.

** Kimberly S. Gibbons: May 19, 1991

<u>REFERENCES</u>

Georgia Department of Education. Quality Core Curriculum: Language Arts—Grades 6th—8th, 1999.

Kimberly Rena Sheffield-Gibbons

ABOUT THE AUTHOR

Kimberly Rena Sheffield Gibbons was born in Douglasville, Georgia to Joe Cephus and Catherine Parker Sheffield. She grew up in Villa Rica, Georgia, the birthplace of the "Father of Gospel," Thomas Dorsey. Gibbons' love for teaching began at an early age as she and her siblings often used their imagination to portray teachers.

Teaching a children's Sunday school class gave Kimberly the opportunity to work with children. After several years of experience working with children, she began to pursue teaching as a career.

Gibbons received her Bachelor of Arts degree in English from West Georgia College in Carrollton, Georgia and a Masters degree in Middle Grades education from State University of West Georgia. Mrs. Gibbons has taught for 8 years in public schools, and she has worked as a private tutor.

Mrs. Gibbons is currently working as an educational consultant. She enjoys public speaking, traveling, reading and writing. Gibbons conducts seminars for teachers, youth groups, civic groups and church groups. Kimberly is a member of the Brinson Hill Baptist Church where she faithfully serves as a Sunday school teacher and a youth advisor. She is married to Herbert Gibbons and the two of them live in Wadley, Georgia.

Printed in the United States
59865LVS00003B/64